CW01667778

OECD Due Diligence Guidance for Responsible Supply Chains of Minerals from Conflict-Affected and High-Risk Areas

OECD
BETTER POLICIES FOR BETTER LIVES

This document and any map included herein are without prejudice to the status of or sovereignty over any territory, to the delimitation of international frontiers and boundaries and to the name of any territory, city or area.

Please cite this publication as:
OECD (2016), *OECD Due Diligence Guidance for Responsible Supply Chains of Minerals from Conflict-Affected and High-Risk Areas: Third Edition*, OECD Publishing, Paris.
http://dx.doi.org/10.1787/9789264252479-en

ISBN 978-92-64-25238-7 (print)
ISBN 978-92-64-25247-9 (PDF)

Photo credits: Cover © Hemera/Thinkstock.com

Corrigenda to OECD publications may be found on line at: *www.oecd.org/publishing/corrigenda*.

© OECD 2016

You can copy, download or print OECD content for your own use, and you can include excerpts from OECD publications, databases and multimedia products in your own documents, presentations, blogs, websites and teaching materials, provided that suitable acknowledgment of OECD as source and copyright owner is given. All requests for public or commercial use and translation rights should be submitted to *rights@oecd.org*. Requests for permission to photocopy portions of this material for public or commercial use shall be addressed directly to the Copyright Clearance Center (CCC) at *info@copyright.com* or the Centre français d'exploitation du droit de copie (CFC) at *contact@cfcopies.com*.

Foreword

The OECD Due Diligence Guidance for Responsible Supply Chains of Minerals from Conflict-Affected and High-Risk Areas *("the Guidance") is the first example of a collaborative government-backed multi-stakeholder initiative on responsible supply chain management of minerals from conflict-affected areas. Its objective is to help companies respect human rights and avoid contributing to conflict through their mineral sourcing practices. The Guidance is also intended to cultivate transparent mineral supply chains and sustainable corporate engagement in the mineral sector with a view to enabling countries to benefit from their mineral resources and preventing the extraction and trade of minerals from becoming a source of conflict, human rights abuses, and insecurity. With its Supplements on Tin, Tantalum, Tungsten and Gold, the OECD Guidance provides companies with a complete package to source minerals responsibly in order for trade in those minerals to support peace and development and not conflict.*

The Guidance was developed through a multi-stakeholder process with in-depth engagement from OECD and eleven countries of the International Conference on the Great Lakes Region (Angola, Burundi, Central African Republic, Republic of Congo, Democratic Republic of Congo, Kenya, Rwanda, Sudan, Tanzania, Uganda and Zambia), industry, civil society, as well as the United Nations Group of Experts on the DRC. Five multi-stakeholder consultations were held to develop the Guidance and its two Supplements, with four in Paris in December 2009 and April 2010 as well as May and November 2011. A joint ICGLR-OECD consultation was held in Nairobi in September 2010 where Brazil, Malaysia and South Africa were also represented. As a result, the Guidance is practically-oriented, with emphasis on collaborative constructive approaches to complex challenges.

The United Nations Security Council resolution 1952 (2010) [S/RES/1952(2010)] supported taking forward the due diligence recommendations contained in the final report of the United Nations Group of Experts on the Democratic Republic of the Congo, designed to be consistent with the OECD Due Diligence Guidance.

The Guidance has been approved by the OECD Investment Committee and the OECD Development Assistance Committee, and has been endorsed by the eleven member states of the International Conference on the Great Lakes Region (ICGLR) in the Lusaka Declaration, adopted on 15 December 2010.

An OECD Recommendation on the Due Diligence Guidance was adopted by Council at Ministerial level on 25 May 2011, amended on 17 July 2012 to include a reference to the Supplement on Gold and again amended on 25 September 2015 following approval by the Investment Committee and the Development Assistance Committee of changes to the Introduction to the Guidance. While not legally binding, the Recommendation reflects the common position and political commitment of OECD members and non-member adherents.

This third edition of the OECD Due Diligence Guidance for Responsible Supply Chains of Minerals from Conflict-Affected and High-Risk Areas *provides clarification on the scope of the Guidance by removing language in the Introduction that was perceived to limit its application only to the supply chains of tin, tantalum, tungsten and gold. The updated edition now clarifies that the Guidance provides a framework for detailed due diligence as a basis for responsible supply chain management of all minerals.*

Table of Contents

Figure

Recommendation of the Council on Due Diligence Guidance for Responsible Supply Chains of Minerals from Conflict-Affected and High-Risk Areas[1]

As amended on 17 July 2012

THE COUNCIL,

Having regard to Article 5(b) of the Convention on the Organisation for Economic Co-operation and Development of 14 December 1960;

Having regard to the Guidelines for Multinational Enterprises which form part of the Declaration on International Investment and Multinational Enterprises;

Recalling that the common aim of governments recommending the observance of the Guidelines for Multinational Enterprises and the development community is to promote principles and standards for responsible business conduct;

Observing that responsible sourcing of minerals has developmental and business dimensions;

Having regard to the Policy Framework for Investment adopted in 2006 which aims to mobilise private investment in a way which supports steady economic growth and sustainable development;

Recalling the work of the Development Assistance Committee in the field of international engagement in fragile states, aimed at avoiding harm when engaging in fragile and conflict-affected environments, including the

1. At the time of adoption, Brazil made the following statement: "In adhering to the present Recommendation Brazil understands that the Due Diligence Guidance has been developed on the basis of the experience in the Great Lakes Region in Africa. Brazil is of the view that companies should take due account of relevant decisions by the United Nations, including resolutions of the UN Security Council, in determining if other zones of operation can be considered to be conflict-affected or high-risk areas."

Principles for Good International Engagement in Fragile States and Situations endorsed at its High Level Meeting on 3-4 April 2007;

Recalling the efforts of the international community to cooperate in the fight against corruption, including through the OECD Convention on Combating Bribery of Foreign Public Officials in International Business Transactions and the United Nations Convention Against Corruption;

Recognising that governments, international organisations and companies can each draw on their respective competences and roles to contribute to ensuring that trade and investment in natural resources is beneficial to society at large;

Considering the efforts of the international community, in particular the International Conference on the Great Lakes Region, to combat illegal exploitation of natural resources in conflict-affected and high-risk areas;

Recognising that there is significant exploitation of natural mineral resources in conflict-affected and high-risk areas and that companies sourcing from or directly operating in those areas may face higher risk of contributing to conflict;

Noting that due diligence for responsible supply chains of minerals from conflict-affected and high-risk areas is an on-going, proactive and reactive process through which companies can ensure that they respect human rights and do not contribute to conflict;

Having regard to the OECD Due Diligence Guidance for Responsible Supply Chains of Minerals from Conflict-Affected and High-Risk Areas (hereafter "the Guidance"), developed in cooperation with the International Conference on the Great Lakes Region and approved by the Investment Committee and the Development Assistance Committee;

Having regard to the Supplement on Tin, Tantalum and Tungsten and the Supplement on Gold, which are an integral part of the Guidance, and noting that supplements on other minerals may be added to the Guidance in the future;

Noting that this Guidance sets out the steps companies should take to identify and address actual or potential risks in order to prevent or mitigate adverse impacts associated with their activities or relationships, while recognising that flexibility is needed in its application depending on individual circumstances and factors such as the size of the enterprise, the location of the activities, the situation in a particular country, the sector and nature of the products or services involved;

Recognising that the serious abuses associated with the extraction, transport or trade in minerals listed in Annex II to this Recommendation, especially when perpetrated against women and children, should not be tolerated;

On the proposal of the Investment Committee in enlarged session (including the non-Member adherents to the Declaration on International Investment and Multinational Enterprises) and the Development Assistance Committee;

RECOMMENDS that Members and non-Member adherents to the Declaration on International Investment and Multinational Enterprises actively promote the observance of the Guidance by companies operating in or from their territories and sourcing minerals from conflict-affected or high-risk areas with the aim of ensuring that they respect human rights, avoid contributing to conflict and successfully contribute to sustainable, equitable and effective development;

RECOMMENDS, in particular, that Members and non-Member adherents to the Declaration on International Investment and Multinational Enterprises take measures to actively support the integration into corporate management systems of the 5-Step Framework for Risk-Based Due Diligence in the Mineral Supply Chain having due regard to the Model Supply Chain Policy set out respectively in Annexes I and II to this Recommendation of which they form an integral part;

RECOMMENDS that Members and non-Member adherents to the Declaration on International Investment and Multinational Enterprises, with the support of the OECD including through its activities with the United Nations and international development organisations, ensure the widest possible dissemination of the Guidance and its active use by other stakeholders including professional associations, financial institutions, and civil society organisations;

INVITES other non-Members to take due account of and adhere to the present Recommendation;

INSTRUCTS the Investment Committee and the Development Assistance Committee to monitor the implementation of the Recommendation and to report to Council no later than three years following its adoption and as appropriate thereafter.

© OECD 2016

OECD Due Diligence Guidance for Responsible Supply Chains of Minerals from Conflict-Affected and High-Risk Areas

Introduction

In conflict-affected and high-risk areas, companies involved in mining and trade in minerals have the potential to generate income, growth and prosperity, sustain livelihoods and foster local development. In such situations, companies may also be at risk of contributing to or being associated with significant adverse impacts, including serious human rights abuses and conflict.

This Guidance provides a framework for detailed due diligence as a basis for responsible global supply chain management of minerals.[1] The purpose of this Guidance is to help companies respect human rights and avoid contributing to conflict through their sourcing decisions, including the choice of their suppliers. By doing so, this Guidance will help companies contribute to sustainable development and source responsibly from conflict-affected and high-risk areas, while creating the enabling conditions for constructive engagement with suppliers. This Guidance is intended to serve as a common reference for all suppliers and other stakeholders in the mineral supply chain and any industry-driven schemes which may be developed, in order to clarify expectations concerning the nature of responsible supply chain management of minerals from conflict-affected and high-risk areas.

This Guidance is the result of a collaborative initiative among governments, international organisations, industry and civil society to promote accountability and transparency in the supply chain of minerals from conflict-affected and high-risk areas.

1. Metals reasonably assumed to be recycled are excluded from the scope of this Guidance. Recycled metals are reclaimed end-user or post-consumer products, or scrap processed metals created during product manufacturing. Recycled metal includes excess, obsolete, defective, and scrap metal materials which contain refined or processed metals that are appropriate to recycle in the production of tin, tantalum, tungsten and/or gold. Minerals partially processed, unprocessed or a bi-product from another ore are not recycled metals.

Conflict-Affected and High-Risk Areas

Conflict-affected and high-risk areas are identified by the presence of armed conflict, widespread violence or other risks of harm to people. Armed conflict may take a variety of forms, such as a conflict of international or non-international character, which may involve two or more states, or may consist of wars of liberation, or insurgencies, civil wars, etc. *High-risk areas* may include areas of political instability or repression, institutional weakness, insecurity, collapse of civil infrastructure and widespread violence. Such areas are often characterised by widespread human rights abuses and violations of national or international law.

What is due diligence in the mineral supply chain and why is it necessary?

Due diligence is an on-going, proactive and reactive process through which companies can ensure that they respect human rights and do not contribute to conflict.[2] Due diligence can also help companies ensure they observe international law and comply with domestic laws, including those governing the illicit trade in minerals and United Nations sanctions. Risk-based due diligence refers to the steps companies should take to identify and address actual or potential risks in order to prevent or mitigate adverse impacts associated with their activities or sourcing decisions.

For the purposes of this Guidance, "risks" are defined in relation to the potentially adverse impacts of a company's operations, which result from a company's own activities or its relationships with third parties, including suppliers and other entities in the supply chain. Adverse impacts may include harm to people (*i.e.* external impacts), or reputational damage or legal liability for the company (*i.e.* internal impacts), or both. Such internal and external impacts are often interdependent, with external harm coupled with reputational damage or exposure to legal liability.

A company assesses risk by identifying the factual circumstances of its activities and relationships and evaluating those facts against relevant standards provided under national and international law, recommendations on responsible business conduct by international organisations, government-backed tools, private sector voluntary initiatives and a company's internal policies and

2. OECD (2011), *OECD Guidelines for Multinational Enterprises*, OECD, Paris; OECD (2006), *OECD Risk Awareness Tool for Multinational Enterprises in Weak Governance Zones*, OECD, Paris; and, *Guiding Principles on Business and Human Rights: Implementing the United Nations "Protect, Respect and Remedy" Framework* (Report of the Special Represantative of the Secretary-General on the Issue of Human Rights and Transnational Corporations and other Business Enterprises, John Ruggie, A/HRC/17/31, 21 March 2011).

systems. This approach also helps to scale the due diligence exercise to the size of the company's activities or supply chain relationships.

Companies may face risks in their mineral supply chains because of circumstances of mineral extraction, trade or handling which *by their nature* have higher risks of significant adverse impacts, such as financing conflict or fuelling, facilitating or exacerbating conditions of conflict. In spite of the fragmented production process in the supply chain, and independent from their position or leverage over suppliers, companies are not insulated from the risk of contributing to or being associated with adverse impacts occurring at various points in the mineral supply chain. Because of this, companies should take reasonable steps and make good faith efforts to conduct due diligence to identify and prevent or mitigate any risks of adverse impacts associated with the conditions of mineral extraction and the relationships of suppliers operating in conflict-affected or high- risk areas.

The Mineral Supply Chain

The process of bringing a raw mineral to the consumer market involves multiple actors and generally includes the extraction, transport, handling, trading, processing, smelting, refining and alloying, manufacturing and sale of end product. The term supply chain refers to the system of all the activities, organisations, actors, technology, information, resources and services involved in moving the mineral from the extraction site downstream to its incorporation in the final product for end consumers.

In practice, due diligence is structured around the steps that companies should take to:

- identify the factual circumstances involved in the extraction, transport, handling, trading, processing, smelting, refining and alloying, manufacturing or selling of products that contain minerals originating from conflict-affected and high-risk areas;
- identify and assess any actual or potential risks by evaluating the factual circumstances against standards set out in the company's supply chain policy (see the Model Supply Chain Policy, Annex II);
- prevent or mitigate the identified risks by adopting and implementing a risk management plan. These may result in a decision to continue trade throughout the course of risk mitigation efforts, temporarily suspend trade while pursuing ongoing risk mitigation, or disengage with a supplier either after failed attempts at mitigation or where the company deems mitigation not feasible or the risks unacceptable.

Who should carry out due diligence?

This Guidance applies to all companies in the mineral supply chain that supply or use minerals sourced from conflict-affected or high-risk areas. While implementation of due diligence should be tailored to particular company activities and relationships, such as their position in the supply chain, all companies should conduct due diligence aimed at ensuring that they do not contribute to human rights abuses or conflict.

This Guidance recognises that due diligence in conflict-affected and high-risk areas presents practical challenges. Flexibility is needed in the application of due diligence. The nature and extent of due diligence that is appropriate will depend on individual circumstances and be affected by factors such as the size of the enterprise, the location of the activities, the situation in a particular country, the sector and nature of the products or services involved. These challenges may be met in a variety of ways, including but not limited to:

- Industry-wide cooperation in building capacity to conduct due diligence.
- Cost-sharing within industry for specific due diligence tasks.
- Participation in initiatives on responsible supply chain management.[3]
- Coordination between industry members who share suppliers.
- Cooperation between upstream and downstream companies.
- Building partnerships with international and civil society organisations.
- Integrating the model supply chain policy (Annex II) and specific due diligence recommendations outlined in this Guidance into existing policies and management systems, due diligence practices of the company, such as procurement practices, integrity and know your customer due diligence measures and sustainability, corporate social responsibility or other annual reporting.

In addition to providing the principles and processes for companies, this Guidance recommends due diligences processes and procedures that emerging industry-wide supply chain initiatives should meet as they work towards conflict-sensitive responsible sourcing practices, and may assist and complement the development and implementation of comprehensive certification schemes, such as the International Conference of the Great Region certification scheme and tools.[4]

3. For example: *ITRI Supply Chain Initiative* (iTSCi); *Conflict-Free Smelter Program* developed by the Electronic Industry Citizenship Coalition (EICC) and Global e-Sustainability Initiative (GeSI); *Conflict-Free Gold Standard*, World Gold Council (2012); and *Chain-of-Custody Certification*, Responsible Jewellery Council (2012); Global Reporting Initiative Supply Chain Working Group (2010).
4. See *ICGLR Regional Initiative against the Illegal Exploitation of Natural Resources*, *www.icglr.org*.

Structure of the Guidance

This Guidance provides 1) an overarching due diligence framework for responsible supply chains of minerals from conflict-affected and high-risk areas (*see* Annex I); 2) a model mineral supply chain policy providing a common set of principles (*see* Annex II); 3) suggested measures for risk mitigation and indicators for measuring improvement which upstream companies may consider with the possible support of downstream companies (*see* Annex III); and 4) two Supplements on tin-tantalum-tungsten and gold tailored to the challenges associated with the structure of the supply chain of these minerals. The Supplements contain specific due diligence recommendations articulated on the basis of companies' different positions and roles in their supply chains. Companies using these minerals, or their refined metal derivates, should first consult the red flags listed in each Supplement to determine if the due diligence processes described therein are applicable.

Nature of the Guidance

This Guidance builds on and is consistent with the principles and standards contained in the OECD Guidelines for Multinational Enterprises and the OECD Risk Awareness Tool for Multinational Enterprises in Weak Governance Zones. It provides recommendations jointly addressed by governments to companies operating in or sourcing minerals from conflict-affected and high-risk areas, providing guidance on principles and due diligence processes for responsible supply chains of minerals from conflict-affected and high-risk areas, consistent with applicable laws and relevant international standards. Observance of this Guidance is voluntary and not legally enforceable.

ANNEX I

Five-Step Framework for Risk-Based Due Diligence in the Mineral Supply Chain

While specific due diligence requirements and processes will differ depending on the mineral and the position of the company in the supply chain (as detailed in the mineral Supplements), companies should review their choice of suppliers and sourcing decisions and integrate into their management systems the following five-step framework for risk-based due diligence for responsible supply chains of minerals from conflict-affected and high-risk areas:

1. ***Establish strong company management systems.*** Companies should:

   A) Adopt, and clearly communicate to suppliers and the public, a company policy for the supply chain of minerals originating from conflict-affected and high-risk areas. This policy should incorporate the standards against which due diligence is to be conducted, consistent with the standards set forth in the model supply chain policy in Annex II.

   B) Structure internal management to support supply chain due diligence.

   C) Establish a system of controls and transparency over the mineral supply chain. This includes a chain of custody or a traceability system or the identification of upstream actors in the supply chain. This may be implemented through participation in industry-driven programs.

   D) Strengthen company engagement with suppliers. A supply chain policy should be incorporated into contracts and/or agreements with suppliers. Where possible, assist suppliers in building capacities with a view to improving due diligence performance.

   E) Establish a company-level, or industry-wide, grievance mechanism as an early-warning risk-awareness system.

2. ***Identify and assess risk in the supply chain.*** Companies should:
   - A) Identify risks in their supply chain as recommended in the Supplements.
   - B) Assess risks of adverse impacts in light of the standards of their supply chain policy consistent with Annex II and the due diligence recommendations in this Guidance.
3. ***Design and implement a strategy to respond to identified risks.*** Companies should:
   - A) Report findings of the supply chain risk assessment to the designated senior management of the company.
   - B) Devise and adopt a risk management plan. Devise a strategy for risk management by either *i)* continuing trade throughout the course of measurable risk mitigation efforts; *ii)* temporarily suspending trade while pursuing ongoing measurable risk mitigation; or *iii)* disengaging with a supplier after failed attempts at mitigation or where a company deems risk mitigation not feasible or unacceptable. To determine the correct strategy, companies should review Annex II (*Model Supply Chain Policy for Responsible Global Supply Chains of Minerals from Conflict-Affected and High-Risk Areas*) and consider their ability to influence, and where necessary take steps to build leverage, over suppliers who can most effectively prevent or mitigate the identified risk. If companies pursue risk mitigation efforts while continuing trade or temporarily suspending trade, they should consult with suppliers and affected stakeholders, including local and central government authorities, international or civil society organisations and affected third parties, where appropriate, and agree on the strategy for measurable risk mitigation in the risk management plan. Companies may draw on the suggested measures and indicators under Annex III of the *Due Diligence Guidance* to design conflict and high-risk sensitive strategies for mitigation in the risk management plan and measure progressive improvement.
   - C) Implement the risk management plan, monitor and track performance of risk mitigation efforts and report back to designated senior management. This may be done in cooperation and/or consultation with local and central government authorities, upstream companies, international or civil society organisations and affected third-parties where the risk management plan is implemented and monitored in conflict-affected and high-risk areas.
   - D) Undertake additional fact and risk assessments for risks requiring mitigation, or after a change of circumstances.

4. ***Carry out independent third-party audit of supply chain due diligence at identified points in the supply chain.*** Companies at identified points (as indicated in the Supplements) in the supply chain should have their due diligence practices audited by independent third parties. Such audits may be verified by an independent institutionalised mechanism.
5. ***Report on supply chain due diligence.*** Companies should publicly report on their supply chain due diligence policies and practices and may do so by expanding the scope of their sustainability, corporate social responsibility or annual reports to cover additional information on mineral supply chain due diligence.

ANNEX II

Model Supply Chain Policy for a Responsible Global Supply Chain of Minerals from Conflict-Affected and High-Risk Areas[1]

Recognising that risks of significant adverse impacts which may be associated with extracting, trading, handling and exporting minerals from conflict-affected and high-risk areas, and recognising that we have the responsibility to respect human rights and not contribute to conflict, we commit to adopt, widely disseminate and incorporate in contracts and/or agreements with suppliers the following policy on responsible sourcing of minerals from conflict-affected and high-risk areas, as representing a common reference for conflict-sensitive sourcing practices and suppliers' risk awareness from the point of extraction until end user. We commit to refraining from any action which contributes to the financing of conflict and we commit to comply with relevant United Nations sanctions resolutions or, where applicable, domestic laws implementing such resolutions.

Regarding serious abuses associated with the extraction, transport or trade of minerals:

1. While sourcing from, or operating in, conflict-affected and high-risk areas, we will neither tolerate nor by any means profit from, contribute to, assist with or facilitate the commission by any party of:

   i) any forms of torture, cruel, inhuman and degrading treatment;

   ii) any forms of forced or compulsory labour, which means work or service which is exacted from any person under the menace of penalty and for which said person has not offered himself voluntarily;

1. This *Model Supply Chain Policy for a Responsible Global Supply Chain of Minerals from Conflict-Affected and High-Risk Areas* is intended to provide a common reference for all actors throughout the entire mineral supply chain. Companies are encouraged to incorporate the model policy into their existing policies on corporate social responsibility, sustainability, or other alternative equivalent.

iii) the worst forms of child labour;[2]

iv) other gross human rights violations and abuses such as widespread sexual violence;

v) war crimes or other serious violations of international humanitarian law, crimes against humanity or genocide.

Regarding risk management of serious abuses:

2. We will immediately suspend or discontinue engagement with upstream suppliers where we identify a reasonable risk that they are sourcing from, or linked to, any party committing serious abuses as defined in paragraph 1.

Regarding direct or indirect support to non-state armed groups:[3]

3. We will not tolerate any direct or indirect support to non-state armed groups through the extraction, transport, trade, handling or export of minerals. "Direct or indirect support" to non-state armed groups through the extraction, transport, trade, handling or export of minerals includes, but is not limited to, procuring minerals from, making payments to or otherwise providing logistical assistance or equipment to, non-state armed groups or their affiliates who:[4]

i) illegally control mine sites or otherwise control transportation routes, points where minerals are traded and upstream actors in the supply chain;[5] and/or

ii) illegally tax or extort[6] money or minerals at points of access to mine sites, along transportation routes or at points where minerals are traded; and/or

iii) illegally tax or extort intermediaries, export companies or international traders.

2. See ILO Convention No. 182 on the Worst Forms of Child Labour (1999).
3. To identify non-state armed groups, companies should refer to relevant UN Security Council resolutions.
4. "Affiliates" includes négociants, consolidators, intermediaries, and others in the supply chain that work directly with armed groups to facilitate the extraction, trade or handling of minerals.
5. "Control" of mines, transportation routes, points where minerals are traded and upstream actors in the supply chain means *i)* overseeing extraction, including by granting access to mine sites and/or coordinating downstream sales to intermediaries, export companies or international traders; *ii)* making recourse to any forms of forced or compulsory labour to mine, transport, trade or sell minerals; or *iii)* acting as a director or officer of, or holding beneficial or other ownership interests in, upstream companies or mines.
6. "Extort" from mines, transportation routes, points where minerals are traded or upstream companies means the demanding, under the threat of violence or any other penalty, and for which the person has not voluntarily offered, sums of money or minerals, often in return for granting access to exploit the mine site, access transportation routes, or to transport, purchase, or sell minerals.

Regarding risk management of direct or indirect support to non-state armed groups:

4. We will immediately suspend or discontinue engagement with upstream suppliers where we identify a reasonable risk that they are sourcing from, or linked to, any party providing direct or indirect support to non-state armed groups as defined in paragraph 3.

Regarding public or private security forces:

5. We agree to eliminate, in accordance with paragraph 10, direct or indirect support to public or private security forces who illegally control mine sites, transportation routes and upstream actors in the supply chain; illegally tax or extort money or minerals at point of access to mine sites, along transportation routes or at points where minerals are traded; or illegally tax or extort intermediaries, export companies or international traders.[7]
6. We recognise that the role of public or private security forces at the mine sites and/or surrounding areas and/or along transportation routes should be solely to maintain the rule of law, including safeguarding human rights, providing security to mine workers, equipment and facilities, and protecting the mine site or transportation routes from interference with legitimate extraction and trade.
7. Where we or any company in our supply chain contract public or private security forces, we commit to or we will require that such security forces will be engaged in accordance with the Voluntary Principles on Security and Human Rights. In particular, we will support or take steps, to adopt screening policies to ensure that individuals or units of security forces that are known to have been responsible for gross human rights abuses will not be hired.
8. We will support efforts, or take steps, to engage with central or local authorities, international organisations and civil society organisations to contribute to workable solutions on how transparency, proportionality and accountability in payments made to public security forces for the provision of security could be improved.
9. We will support efforts, or take steps, to engage with local authorities, international organisations and civil society organisations to avoid or minimise the exposure of vulnerable groups, in particular, artisanal miners

7. "Direct or indirect support" does not refer to legally required forms of support, including legal taxes, fees, and/or royalties that companies pay to the government of a country in which they operate (see paragraph 13 below on disclosure of such payments).

where minerals in the supply chain are extracted through artisanal or small-scale mining, to adverse impacts associated with the presence of security forces, public or private, on mine sites.

Regarding risk management of public or private security forces:

10. In accordance with the specific position of the company in the supply chain, we will immediately devise, adopt and implement a risk management plan with upstream suppliers and other stakeholders to prevent or mitigate the risk of direct or indirect support to public or private security forces, as identified in paragraph 5, where we identify that such a reasonable risk exists. In such cases, we will suspend or discontinue engagement with upstream suppliers after failed attempts at mitigation within six months from the adoption of the risk management plan.[8] Where we identify a reasonable risk of activities inconsistent with paragraphs 8 and 9, we will respond in the same vein.

Regarding bribery and fraudulent misrepresentation of the origin of minerals:

11. We will not offer, promise, give or demand any bribes, and will resist the solicitation of bribes to conceal or disguise the origin of minerals, to misrepresent taxes, fees and royalties paid to governments for the purposes of mineral extraction, trade, handling, transport and export.[9]

Regarding money laundering:

12. We will support efforts, or take steps, to contribute to the effective elimination of money laundering where we identify a reasonable risk of money-laundering resulting from, or connected to, the extraction, trade, handling, transport or export of minerals derived from the illegal taxation or extortion of minerals at points of access to mine sites, along transportation routes or at points where minerals are traded by upstream suppliers.

8. As detailed in Step 3(D) of Annex I, companies should conduct an additional risk assessment on those risks requiring mitigation after the adoption of the risk management plan. If within six months from the adoption of the risk management plan there is no significant measurable improvement to prevent or mitigate the risk of direct or indirect support to public or private security forces, as identified in paragraph 5, companies should suspend or discontinue engagement with the supplier for a minimum of three months. Suspension may be accompanied by a revised risk management plan, stating the performance objectives for progressive improvement that should be met before resuming the trade relationship.
9. *See* OECD Convention on Combating Bribery of Foreign Public Officials in International Business Transactions (1997); and the United Nations Convention Against Corruption (2004).

Regarding the payment of taxes, fees and royalties due to governments:

13. We will ensure that all taxes, fees, and royalties related to mineral extraction, trade and export from conflict-affected and high-risk areas are paid to governments and, in accordance with the company's position in the supply chain, we commit to disclose such payments in accordance with the principles set forth under the Extractive Industry Transparency Initiative (EITI).

Regarding risk management of bribery and fraudulent misrepresentation of the origin of minerals, money-laundering and payment of taxes, fees and royalties to governments:

14. In accordance with the specific position of the company in the supply chain, we commit to engage with suppliers, central or local governmental authorities, international organisations, civil society and affected third parties, as appropriate, to improve and track performance with a view to preventing or mitigating risks of adverse impacts through measureable steps taken in reasonable timescales. We will suspend or discontinue engagement with upstream suppliers after failed attempts at mitigation.[10]

10. As detailed in Step 3(D) of Annex I, companies should conduct an additional risk assessment on those risks requiring mitigation after the adoption of the risk management plan. If within six months from the adoption of the risk management plan there is no significant measurable improvement to prevent or mitigate the risks of bribery and fraudulent misrepresentation of the origin of minerals, money-laundering and payment of taxes, fees and royalties to governments, companies should suspend or discontinue engagement with the supplier for a minimum of three months. Suspension may be accompanied by a revised risk management plan, stating the performance objectives for progressive improvement that should be met before resuming the trade relationship.

ANNEX III

Suggested Measures for Risk Mitigation and Indicators for Measuring Improvement

SUPPLY CHAIN POLICY – SECURITY AND RELATED ISSUES

RISK MITIGATION:

The following suggested risk mitigation measures may be considered for implementation by upstream companies individually or through associations, joint assessment teams or other suitable means to undertake the following activities:

- alert relevant central government authority (*e.g.* Ministry of Mines) of abusive and exploitative practices occurring in the supply chain;
- in areas in which minerals are illegally taxed or extorted, take immediate steps to ensure that upstream intermediaries and consolidators disclose downstream or publicly the payments made to public or private security forces for the provision of security;
- engage with intermediaries and consolidators to help build their capabilities to document the behaviour of security and payments to security forces;
- while sourcing from areas of artisanal and small-scale mining ("ASM"), support the formalisation of security arrangements between ASM communities, local government, and public or private security forces, in cooperation with civil society and international organisations, as appropriate, to ensure that all payments are freely made and proportionate to the service provided, clarify rules of engagement consistent with the Voluntary Principles on Security and Human Rights, the UN Code of Conduct for Law Enforcement Officials and the UN Basic Principles on the Use of Force and Firearms by Law Enforcement Officials;

SUPPLY CHAIN POLICY – SECURITY AND RELATED ISSUES *(cont.)*

- support the establishment of community forums to share and communicate information;
- support the establishment of a trust or other similar fund, where appropriate, through which security forces are paid for their services;
- build partnership with international organisations or civil society organisations, as appropriate, to support capacity-building of security forces consistent with the Voluntary Principles on Security and Human Rights, on mine sites, and UN Code of Conduct for Law Enforcement Officials or the UN Basic Principles on the Use of Force and Firearms by Law Enforcement Officials.

For further guidance, *see* Multilateral Investment Guarantee Agency, *The Voluntary Principles on Security and Human Rights: An Implementation Toolkit for Major Sites* (2008); International Committee of the Red Cross – Training Resources for armed police and security personnel; and the *International Code of Conduct for Private Security Service Providers* (2010).

RECOMMENDED INDICATORS FOR MEASURING IMPROVEMENT: *See*, for example, Global Reporting Initiative, Indicator Protocols Set: Human Rights, Mining and Metals Sector Supplement (Version 3.0), indicator **HR8:** "*Percentage of security personnel trained in the organisation's policies or procedures concerning aspects of human rights that are relevant to operations*". For further descriptions of indicators, see the commentaries to the indicator. For guidance on reporting on indicators and compiling relevant information, including with regard to risks to communities and women, *see* Global Reporting Initiative, Sustainability Reporting Guidelines and GRI Mining and Metals Sector Supplement (Version 3.0).

With regard to minerals originating from mines or transported along transportation routes where security forces are present, *the percentage of minerals or money, on a disaggregate per batch basis, illegally taxed or extorted from upstream actors by public or private security forces; the nature and type of payments to public or private security, including the nature and type of any arrangement on the provision of security and payment.*

SUPPLY CHAIN POLICY – SECURITY AND EXPOSURE OF ARTISANAL MINERS TO ADVERSE IMPACTS

RISK MITIGATION:

When sourcing from areas of artisanal mining, the following suggested risk mitigation measures may be considered for implementation by upstream companies individually or through associations, joint assessment teams or other suitable means to undertake the following activities:

- minimise the risk of exposure of artisanal miners to abusive practices, by supporting host countries governments' efforts for the progressive professionalization and formalisation of the artisanal sector, through the establishment of cooperatives, associations or other membership structures.

For further guidance on how to carry out this risk mitigation, *see* Responsible Jewellery Council, *Standards Guidance*, "COP 2.14 Artisanal and Small-Scale Mining", including "supporting the wider community by locally sourcing the provision of as many goods and services as possible; eliminating child labour as a condition of engagement in the community; improving women's conditions in ASM communities through gender awareness and empowerment programs."

RECOMMENDED INDICATORS FOR MEASURING IMPROVEMENT: *See*, for example, Global Reporting Initiative, Indicator Protocols Set: Society, Mining and Metals Sector Supplement (Version 3.0), indicator **MM8:** "*Number (and percentage) of [...] operating sites where artisanal and small-scale mining (ASM) takes place on, or adjacent to, the site; the associated risks and the actions taken to manage and mitigate these risks*". For further descriptions of indicators, see the commentaries to the indicator. For guidance on reporting on indicators and compiling relevant information, including risks to communities and women, *see* Global Reporting Initiative, Sustainability Reporting Guidelines and Mining and Metals Sector Supplement (Version 3.0).

SUPPLY CHAIN POLICY – BRIBERY AND FRAUDULENT MISREPRESENTATION OF MINERALS ORIGIN

RISK MITIGATION:

Upstream companies may cooperate through associations, assessment teams or other suitable means to build capabilities of suppliers, in particular SMEs, to conduct due diligence for responsible supply chains of minerals from conflict-affected and high-risk areas.

RECOMMENDED INDICATORS FOR MEASURING IMPROVEMENT: Indicators for improvement should be based on the processes contained in the Guidance. For example, indicators may include *the information disclosed downstream; the nature of chain of custody or supply chain transparency systems in place; the nature and form of supply chain risk assessments and management, in particular to verify information generated by chain of custody and transparency systems; the engagement of the company in capability training and/or other industry initiatives for supply chain due diligence.*

SUPPLY CHAIN POLICY – MONEY LAUNDERING

RISK MITIGATION:

The following suggested risk mitigation measures may be considered for implementation by upstream companies individually or through associations, joint assessment teams or other suitable means to undertake the following activities:

- develop supplier, customer and transactional red flags to identify suspicious behaviour and activities;
- identify and verify the identity of all suppliers, business partners and customers;
- report suspicious behaviour of criminal activity to local, national, regional and international law enforcement agencies.

For further guidance, *see* Financial Action Task Force, Guidance on the risk-based approach to combating money laundering and terrorist financing.

RECOMMENDED INDICATORS FOR MEASURING IMPROVEMENT: Indicators for improvement should be based on the processes contained in the Guidance. For example, potential indicators may include *the supply chain policy; the information disclosed downstream, the nature of chain of custody or supply chain transparency system in place; the nature and form of supply chain risk assessments and management, in particular to verify information generated by chain of custody and transparency systems; the engagement of the company in capability training and/or other industry initiatives for supply chain due diligence.*

SUPPLY CHAIN POLICY – TRANSPARENCY ON TAXES, FEES AND ROYALTIES PAID TO GOVERNMENTS

RISK MITIGATION:

The following suggested risk mitigation measures may be considered for implementation by upstream companies individually or through associations, assessment teams or other suitable means to undertake the following activities:

- support the implementation of the Extractive Industry Transparency Initiative;
- support the public disclosure, on a disaggregate basis, of all information on taxes, fees, and royalties that are paid to governments for the purposes of mineral extraction, trade, and export from conflict-affected and high-risk areas;
- inform relevant local and central governmental agencies of potential weaknesses in revenue collection and monitoring;
- support capability training of these agencies to effectively carry out their duties.

For a guide on how business can support EITI, see *http://eiti.org/document/businessguide*.

RECOMMENDED INDICATORS FOR MEASURING IMPROVEMENT: *See*, for example, Global Reporting Initiative, Indicator Protocols Set: Economic, Mining and Metals Sector Supplement (Version 3.0), indicator **EC1:** "*Direct economic value generated and distributed, including revenues, operating costs, employee compensation, donations and other community investments, retained earnings, and payments to capital providers and governments*". For further descriptions of indicators, see the commentaries to the indicator. For guidance on reporting on indicators and compiling relevant information, *see* Global Reporting Initiative, Sustainability Reporting Guidelines and Mining and Metals Sector Supplement (Version 3.0).

OECD Due Diligence Guidance for Responsible Supply Chains
of Minerals from Conflict-Affected and High-Risk Areas
© OECD 2016

Supplement on Tin, Tantalum and Tungsten

Scope and definitions

This Supplement provides specific guidance on supply chain due diligence of tin, tantalum and tungsten (hereinafter minerals) from conflict-affected or high-risk areas according to the different positions in the mineral supply chain. It distinguishes between the roles of and the corresponding due diligence recommendations addressed to *upstream companies* and *downstream companies* in the supply chain.

For the purposes of this Supplement, "upstream" means the mineral supply chain from the mine to smelters/refiners. "Upstream companies" include miners (artisanal and small-scale or large-scale producers),[1] local traders or exporters from the country of mineral origin, international concentrate traders, mineral re-processors and smelters/refiners. The *OECD Due Diligence Guidance for Responsible Supply Chains of Minerals from Conflict-Affected and High-Risk Areas* and this *Supplement on Tin, Tantalum and Tungsten* (hereafter "Guidance"), recommends, among other things, that these companies establish a system of internal control over the minerals in their possession (chain of custody or traceability) and establish on-the-ground assessment teams, which may be set up jointly through cooperation among upstream companies while retaining individual responsibility, for generating and sharing verifiable, reliable, up-to-date information on the qualitative circumstances of mineral extraction, trade, handling and export from conflict-affected and high-risk areas. This Guidance calls on these upstream companies to provide the results of risk assessments to their downstream purchasers and have the smelters/refiners' due diligence practices audited by independent third parties, including through an institutionalised mechanism.

1. "Upstream companies" includes artisanal or small-scale producing *enterprises*, rather than individuals or informal working groups of artisanal miners.

"Downstream" means the minerals supply chain from smelters/refiners to retailers. "Downstream companies" include metal traders and exchanges, component manufacturers, product manufacturers, original equipment manufacturers (OEMs) and retailers. The Guidance recommends, among other things, that downstream companies identify, to the best of their efforts, and review the due diligence process of the smelters/refiners in their supply chain and assess whether they adhere to due diligence measures put forward in this Guidance. Downstream companies may participate in industry-wide schemes that assess smelters/refiners' compliance with this Guidance and may draw on the information these schemes provide to help them fulfil the recommendations in this Guidance.

This distinction reflects the fact that internal control mechanisms based on tracing minerals in a company's possession are generally unfeasible after smelting, with refined metals entering the consumer market as small parts of various components in end products. By virtue of these practical difficulties, downstream companies should establish internal controls over their immediate suppliers and may coordinate efforts through industry-wide initiatives to build leverage over sub-suppliers, overcome practical challenges and effectively discharge the due diligence recommendations contained in this Guidance.

Red flags triggering the application of this supplement

This Guidance applies to actors operating in a conflict-affected and high-risk area, or potentially supplying or using tin (cassiterite), tantalum (tantalite) or tungsten (wolframite), or their smelted derivates, from a conflict-affected and high-risk area. Companies should preliminarily review their mineral or metal sourcing practices to determine if the Guidance applies to them. The following red flags should trigger the due diligence standards and processes contained in this Guidance:

Red flag locations of mineral origin and transit:

- *The minerals originate from or have been transported via a conflict-affected or high-risk area.*[2]
- *The minerals are claimed to originate from a country that has limited known reserves, likely resources or expected production levels of the mineral in question (i.e. the declared volumes of mineral from that country are out of keeping with its known reserves or expected production levels).*
- *The minerals are claimed to originate from a country in which minerals from conflict-affected and high-risk areas are known to transit.*

2. See Guidance for definition and indicators of conflict-affected and high-risk areas.

Supplier red flags:

The company's suppliers or other known upstream companies have shareholder or other interests in companies that supply minerals from or operate in one of the above-mentioned red flag locations of mineral origin and transit.

The company's suppliers' or other known upstream companies are known to have sourced minerals from a red flag location of mineral origin and transit in the last 12 months.

If a company in the supply chain is unable to determine whether the minerals in the company's possession come from a "red flag location of mineral origin or transit", it should proceed to Step 1 of the Guidance.

Figure 1. **Risks in the supply chain of tin, tantalum and tungsten from conflict-affected and high-risk areas**

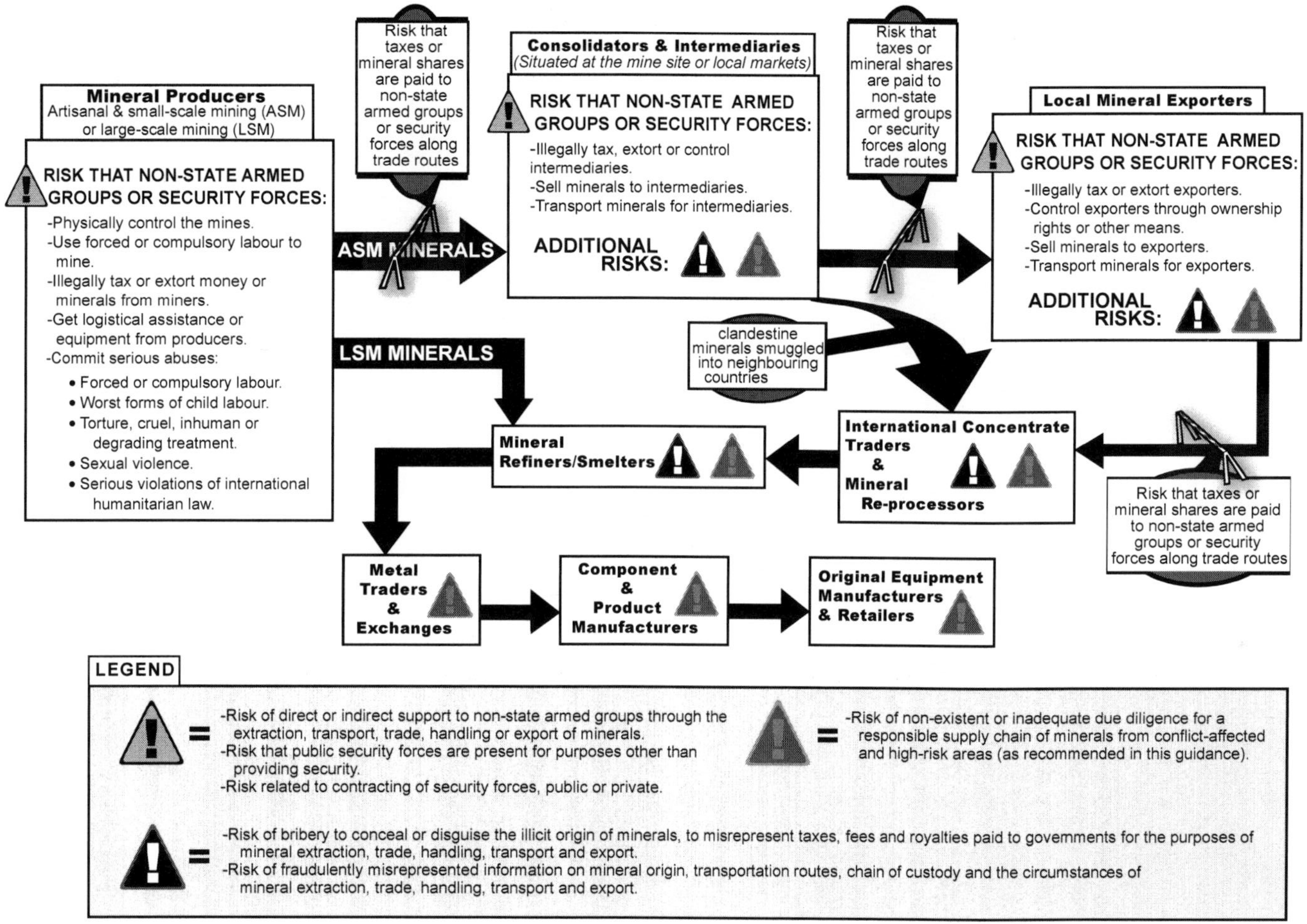

STEP 1: ESTABLISH STRONG COMPANY MANAGEMENT SYSTEMS

OBJECTIVE: To ensure that existing due diligence and management systems within companies address risks associated with minerals from conflict affected or high-risk areas.

A. Adopt and commit to a supply chain policy for minerals originating from conflict-affected and high-risk areas. This policy, for all companies in the supply chain, should include:

1. A policy commitment setting forth principles for common reference on mineral extraction, transport, handling, trading, processing, smelting, refining and alloying, and export, against which the company will assess itself and the activities and relationships of suppliers. This policy should be consistent with the standards set forth in the model supply chain policy in Annex II.
2. A clear and coherent management process to ensure risks are adequately managed. The company should commit to the due diligence steps and recommendations outlined for the various levels identified in this Guidance.

B. Structure internal management systems to support supply chain due diligence. Companies in the supply chain should:

1. Assign authority and responsibility to senior staff with the necessary competence, knowledge and experience to oversee the supply chain due diligence process.
2. Ensure availability of resources necessary to support the operation and monitoring of these processes.[3]
3. Put in place an organisational structure and communication processes that will ensure critical information, including the company policy, reaches relevant employees and suppliers.
4. Ensure internal accountability with respect to the implementation of the supply chain due diligence process.

3. Art. 4.1 (d), ISO 9001:2008.

C. Establish a system of controls and transparency over the mineral supply chain.

C.1. SPECIFIC RECOMMENDATIONS – *For local mineral exporters*

1. Collect[4] and disclose the following information to immediate downstream purchasers, who will then pass them down the supply chain, and to any institutionalised mechanism, regional or global, once in place with the mandate to collect and process information on minerals from conflict-affected and high-risk areas:

   a) all taxes, fees or royalties paid to government for the purposes of extraction, trade, transport and export of minerals;

   b) any other payments made to governmental officials for the purposes of extraction, trade, transport and export of minerals;

   c) all taxes and any other payments made to public or private security forces or other armed groups at all points in the supply chain from extraction onwards;

   d) the ownership (including beneficial ownership) and corporate structure of the exporter, including the names of corporate officers and directors; the business, government, political or military affiliations of the company and officers;

   e) the mine of mineral origin;

   f) quantity, dates and method of extraction (artisanal and small-scale or large-scale mining);

   g) locations where minerals are consolidated, traded, processed or upgraded;

   h) the identification of all upstream intermediaries, consolidators or other actors in the upstream supply chain;

   i) transportation routes.

4. Due diligence is an on-going, proactive and reactive process, and therefore information may be collected and progressively built with the quality progressively improved through various steps in the Guidance, including through supplier communication [such as through contractual provisions or other processes described in Step 1(C) and Step 1(D)], through established chain of custody or transparency systems [*see* Step 1(C.4)], and through risk assessments [see Step 2(I) and Appendix: Guiding Note for Upstream Company Risk Assessment].

C.2. SPECIFIC RECOMMENDATIONS – *For international concentrate traders and mineral re-processors:*

1. Incorporate the above disclosure requirements into commercial contracts with local exporters.[5]
2. Collect and disclose the following information to immediate downstream purchasers and to any institutionalised mechanism, regional or global, once in place with the mandate to collect and process information on minerals from conflict-affected and high-risk areas:
   a) all export, import and re-export documentation, including records of all payments given for the purposes of export, import and re-export and all taxes and any other payments made to public or private security forces or other armed groups;
   b) the identification of all immediate suppliers (local exporters);
   c) all information provided by local exporter.

C.3. SPECIFIC RECOMMENDATIONS – *For smelters/refiners:*

1. Incorporate the above disclosure requirements into commercial contracts with international concentrate traders, mineral re-processors and local exporters.[6]
2. Maintain the information generated by the chain of custody and/or traceability system outlined below for a minimum of five years,[7] preferably on a computerised database and make it available to downstream purchasers and to any institutionalised mechanism, regional or global, once in place with the mandate to collect and process information on minerals from conflict-affected and high-risk areas.

C.4. SPECIFIC RECOMMENDATIONS – *For all upstream companies:*

1. Introduce a chain of custody and/or traceability system that generates the following information on a disaggregated basis for the minerals from a "red flag location of mineral origin and transit", preferably supported by documentation: mine of mineral origin; quantity and dates of extraction; locations where minerals are consolidated, traded or processed; all taxes, fees, royalties or other payments made to governmental officials for the purposes of extraction, trade, transport and export of minerals; all taxes

5. It is the responsibility of the international concentrate trader to gain and maintain the information requested from local exporters regardless of whether exporters comply with the recommendations above.
6. It is the responsibility of the smelter/refiner to gain and maintain the information requested from international concentrate traders and local exporters regardless of whether they comply with the recommendations above.
7. See FATF Recommendation 10. Also see Annex II, Kimberley Process Certification Scheme and Kimberley Process Moscow Declaration.

and other payments made to public or private security forces or other armed groups; identification of all actors in the upstream supply chain; transportation routes.[8]

2. Make all information gained and maintained pursuant to the due diligence standards and processes contained in this Guidance available to downstream purchasers and auditors and to any institutionalised mechanism, regional or global, once in place with the mandate to collect and process information on minerals from conflict-affected and high-risk areas.
3. Avoid, where practicable, cash purchases and ensure that all unavoidable cash purchases of minerals are supported by verifiable documentation and preferably routed through official banking channels.[9]
4. Support the implementation of the principles and criteria set forth under the Extractive Industry Transparency Initiative (EITI).[10]

C.5. *SPECIFIC RECOMMENDATIONS – For all downstream companies:*

1. Introduce a supply chain transparency system that allows the identification of the smelters/refiners in the company's mineral supply chain through which the following information on the supply chain of minerals from "red flag locations of mineral origin and transit" should be obtained: the identification of all countries of origin, transport and transit for the minerals in the supply chains of each smelter/refiner. Companies which, due to their size or other factors, may find it difficult to identify actors upstream from their direct suppliers may engage and actively cooperate with industry members with whom they share suppliers or downstream companies with whom they have a business relationship to identify which smelters are in the supply chain.
2. Maintain related records for a minimum of five years, preferably on a computerised database.
3. Support extending digital information-sharing systems on suppliers[11] to include smelters/refiners, and adapt systems to assess supplier due diligence in the supply chain of minerals from conflict-affected and high-risk areas,

8. See ITRI Supply Chain Initiative (iTSCi).
9. Financial institutions are encouraged to refer to this Guidance and supplement when undertaking customer due diligence for the purposes of providing their services and factor their compliance with this Guidance into their decision-making.
10. For information on the EITI, see *http://eiti.org/*. For a guide on how business can support EITI, see *http://eiti.org/document/businessguide*.
11. For example, see digital supplier information systems such as E.TASC.

utilizing the criteria and process recommended in this Guidance, with due regard to business confidentiality and other competitive concerns.[12]

D. Strengthen company engagement with suppliers. Companies in the supply chain should ensure that suppliers commit to a supply chain policy consistent with Annex II and the due diligence processes in this Guidance. In order to do this, the company should:

1. Establish, where practicable, long-term relationships with suppliers as opposed to short-term or one-off contracts in order to build leverage over suppliers.
2. Communicate to suppliers their expectations on responsible supply chains of minerals from conflict-affected and high-risk areas, and incorporate the supply chain policy and due diligence processes set out in this Guidance into commercial contracts and/or written agreements with suppliers which can be applied and monitored,[13] including, if deemed necessary, the right to conduct unannounced spot-checks on suppliers and have access to their documentation.
3. Consider ways to support and build capabilities of suppliers to improve performance and conform to company supply chain policy.[14]
4. Commit to designing measurable improvement plans with suppliers with the involvement, if relevant and where appropriate, of local and central governments, international organisations and civil society when pursuing risk mitigation.[15]

E. Establish a company level grievance mechanism. Depending on their position in the supply chain companies may:

1. Develop a mechanism allowing any interested party (affected persons or whistle-blowers) to voice concerns regarding the circumstances of mineral extraction, trade, handling and export in a conflict-affected and high-risk area. This will allow a company to be alerted of risks in its supply chain as to the problems in addition to the company fact and risk assessments.
2. Provide such a mechanism directly, or through collaborative arrangements with other companies or organisations, or by facilitating recourse to an external expert or body (*i.e.* ombudsman).

12. Business confidentiality and other competitive concerns means price information and supplier relationships without prejudice to subsequent evolving interpretation. All information will be disclosed to any institutionalised mechanism, regional or global, once in place with the mandate to collect and process information on minerals from conflict-affected and high-risk areas.
13. See Steps 2-5 for information on monitoring suppliers and managing non-compliance.
14. See Step 3, "Risk Mitigation".
15. See Step 3, "Risk Mitigation".

STEP 2: IDENTIFY AND ASSESS RISKS IN THE SUPPLY CHAIN

OBJECTIVE: To identify and assess risks on the circumstances of extraction, trading, handling and export of minerals from conflict-affected and high-risk areas.

I. UPSTREAM COMPANIES

Upstream companies are expected to clarify chain of custody and the circumstances of mineral extraction, trade, handling and export and identify and assess risk by evaluating those circumstances against the model supply chain policy on minerals from conflict-affected and high-risk areas in Annex II. *Upstream companies may cooperate to carry out the recommendations in this section through joint initiatives. However, companies retain individual responsibility for their due diligence, and should ensure that all joint work duly takes into consideration circumstances specific to the individual company.*

A. **Identify the scope of the risk assessment of the mineral supply chain.** Smelters/refiners, international concentrate traders and mineral re-processors should review information generated in Step 1 in order to target risk assessments on those minerals and suppliers triggered by the "red flag locations of mineral origin and transit" and "supplier red flags", as listed in the introduction.

B. **Map the factual circumstances of the company's supply chain(s), under way and planned.** Upstream companies should assess the context of conflict-affected and high-risk areas; clarify the chain of custody, the activities and relationships of all upstream suppliers; and identify the locations and qualitative conditions of the extraction, trade, handling and export of the mineral. Upstream companies should rely on information collected and maintained through Step 1, and should gain and maintain up-to-date on-the-ground information in order to map the supply chain and assess risk effectively. See **Appendix: Guiding Note for Upstream Company Risk Assessments**, which contains guidance on establishing on-the-ground assessment teams (hereafter "assessment teams") and includes a recommended list of questions for consideration. Assessment teams may be established jointly by upstream companies operating or supplying from conflict affected or high-risk areas. Upstream companies will remain individually responsible for following any of the recommendations put forward by assessment teams and acting on them.

C. Assess risks in the supply chain. The company should assess the factual circumstances of the supply chain against the model supply chain policy on a qualitative basis to determine risks in the supply chain:

1. Review applicable standards, including:
   a) The principles and standards of the company supply chain policy, consistent with Annex II.[16]
   b) National laws of the countries where the company is domiciled or publicly-traded (if applicable); of the countries from which the minerals are likely to originate; and of transit or re-export countries.
   c) Legal instruments governing company operations and business relations, such as financing agreements, contractor agreements, and supplier agreements.
   d) Other relevant international instruments, such as the OECD Guidelines for Multinational Enterprises, international human rights and humanitarian law.
2. Determine whether the circumstances in the supply chain (in particular, the answers to the recommended guiding questions outlined in the Appendix) meet the relevant standards. Any reasonable inconsistency between a factual circumstance and a standard should be considered a risk with potential adverse impacts.

II. DOWNSTREAM COMPANIES

Downstream companies should identify the risks in their supply chain by assessing the due diligence practices of their smelters/refiners against this Guidance. Downstream companies who may find it difficult to identify actors upstream from their direct suppliers (due to their size or other factors), may engage and actively cooperate with other industry members with whom they share suppliers or downstream companies with whom they have a business relationship to carry out the recommendation in this section in order to identify the smelters/refiners in their supply chain and assess their due diligence practices or identify through industry validation schemes the refiners/ smelters that meet the requirements of this Guidance in order to source therefrom.[17] Downstream companies retain individual responsibility for their due diligence, and should ensure that all joint work duly takes into consideration circumstances specific to the individual company.

16. See Step 1 (A) above and Annex II.
17. See the Conflict-Free Smelter Program, *www.conflictfreesourcing.org*.

A. Identify, to the best of their efforts, the smelters/refiners in their supply chain. Downstream companies should aim to identify the mineral smelters/refiners that produce the refined metals used in their supply chain. This may be carried out through confidential discussions with the companies' immediate suppliers, through the incorporation of confidential supplier disclosure requirements into supplier contracts, by specifying to direct suppliers the smelters/refiners that meet the requirements of this Guidance, by using confidential information-sharing systems on suppliers and/or through industry wide schemes to disclose upstream actors in the supply chain.[18]

B. Identify the scope of the risk assessment of the mineral supply chain. After identifying the smelters/refiners that produce the refined metal used in their supply chain, downstream companies should engage with those smelters/refiners in their supply chains and obtain from them initial information on country of mineral origin, transit and transportation routes used between mine and smelters/refiners. Downstream companies should review this information and any information generated in Step 1 in order to target risk assessments on those minerals and suppliers triggered by the "red flag locations of mineral origin and transit" and "supplier red flags", as listed in the introduction.

C. Assess whether the smelters/refiners have carried out all elements of due diligence for responsible supply chains of minerals from conflict-affected and high-risk areas.

1. Gain evidence on due diligence practices of the smelter/refiner.
2. Review the information generated by the assessment team.[19]
3. Cross-check evidence of due diligence practices of the smelter/refiner against the supply chain policy and due diligence processes contained in this Guidance.
4. Work with the smelter/refiner and contribute to finding ways to build capacity, mitigate risk and improve due diligence performance, including through industry-wide initiatives.

D. Where necessary, carry out, including through participation in industry-driven programs, joint spot checks at the mineral smelter/refiner's own facilities.

18. See Step 1(C) ("Establish internal controls over the mineral supply chain") and Step 1 (D) above.
19. See Appendix: Guiding Note for Upstream Company Risk Assessment.

STEP 3: DESIGN AND IMPLEMENT A STRATEGY TO RESPOND TO IDENTIFIED RISKS

OBJECTIVE: To evaluate and respond to identified risks in order to prevent or mitigate adverse impacts. Companies may cooperate to carry out the recommendations in this section through joint initiatives. However, companies retain individual responsibility for their due diligence, and should ensure that all joint work duly takes into consideration circumstances specific to the individual company.

A. Report findings to designated senior management, outlining the information gathered and the actual and potential risks identified in the supply chain risk assessment.

B. Devise and adopt a risk management plan. Companies should adopt a supply chain risk management plan that outlines the company responses to risks identified in Step 2. Companies may manage risk by either *i)* continuing trade throughout the course of measurable risk mitigation efforts; *ii)* temporarily suspending trade while pursuing ongoing measurable risk mitigation; or *iii)* disengaging with a supplier in cases where mitigation appears not feasible or unacceptable. To adopt the risk management plan and determine the correct risk management strategy, companies should:

1. *Review the model supply chain policy on minerals from conflict-affected and high-risk areas in* Annex II *or their own internal policy if consistent with* Annex II *to determine whether the identified risks can be mitigated by continuing, suspending or terminating the relationship with suppliers.*
2. *Manage risks that do not require termination of the relationship with a supplier through measurable risk mitigation.* Measurable risk mitigation should aim to promote progressive performance improvement within reasonable timescales. In devising a strategy for risk mitigation, companies should:
   a) Consider, and where necessary take steps to build leverage over upstream suppliers who can most effectively prevent or mitigate the identified risk:
      i) **UPSTREAM COMPANIES** – Depending on their position in the supply chain, upstream companies have significant actual or potential leverage over the actors in the supply chain who can most effectively and most directly mitigate the substantive risks of adverse impacts. If upstream companies decide to pursue risk mitigation while continuing trade or temporarily suspending trade, mitigation efforts should focus on finding ways to

constructively engage, as appropriate, with relevant stakeholders with a view to progressively eliminating the adverse impacts within reasonable timescales.[20]

ii) **DOWNSTREAM COMPANIES** – Depending on their position in the supply chain, downstream companies are encouraged to build and/ or exercise their leverage over upstream suppliers who can most effectively and most directly mitigate the risks of adverse impacts. Should downstream companies decide to pursue risk mitigation while continuing trade or temporarily suspending trade, their mitigation efforts should focus on suppliers' value orientation and capability-training to enable them to conduct and improve due diligence performance. Companies should encourage their industry membership organisations to develop and implement due diligence capability-training modules in cooperation with relevant international organisations, NGOs, stakeholders and other experts.

b) Consult with suppliers and affected stakeholders and agree on the strategy for measurable risk mitigation in the risk management plan. Measurable risk mitigation should be adjusted to the company's specific suppliers and the contexts of their operations, state clear performance objectives within a reasonable timeframe and include qualitative and/or quantitative indicators to measure improvement.

i) **UPSTREAM COMPANIES** – Publish the supply chain risk assessment and the supply chain management plan, with due regard to business confidentiality and other competitive concerns,[21] and make them available to local and central authorities, upstream companies, local civil society and affected third parties. Companies should ensure sufficient time for affected stakeholders to review the risk assessment and management plan and respond to and take due account of questions, concerns and alternative suggestions for risk management.

20. Companies should refer to Annex II for the recommended risk management strategy. Annex III includes suggested measures for risk mitigation and some recommended indicators to measure improvement. More detailed guidance on risk mitigation is expected to come from the implementation phase of the Guidance.
21. See footnote 12.

C. Implement the risk management plan, monitor and track performance of risk mitigation, report back to designated senior management and consider suspending or discontinuing engagement with a supplier after failed attempts at mitigation.

1. **UPSTREAM COMPANIES** – Upstream companies should implement, monitor and track performance of risk mitigation in cooperation and/or consultation with local and central authorities, upstream companies, international or civil society organisations and affected third parties. Upstream companies may wish to establish or support the creation of community-monitoring networks to monitor or track performance of risk mitigation.

D. Undertake additional fact and risk assessments for risks requiring mitigation, or after a change of circumstances.[22] Supply chain due diligence is a dynamic process and requires on-going risk monitoring. After implementing a risk mitigation strategy, companies should repeat Step 2 to ensure effective management of risk. Additionally, any change in the company's supply chain may require some steps to be repeated in order to prevent or mitigate adverse impacts.

22. A change of circumstances should be determined on a risk-sensitive basis through on-going monitoring of the companies' chain of custody documentation and the contexts of the conflict-affected areas of mineral origin and transport. Such change of circumstances may include a change of supplier or actor in the chain of custody, place of origin, transportation routes or point of export. It may also include factors specific to the context, such as an increase in conflict in specific areas, changes in military personnel overseeing an area and ownership or control changes in the mine of origin.

STEP 4: CARRY OUT INDEPENDENT THIRD-PARTY AUDIT OF SMELTER/REFINER'S DUE DILIGENCE PRACTICES

OBJECTIVE: To carry out an independent third-party audit of the smelter/refiner's due diligence for responsible supply chains of minerals from conflict-affected and high-risk areas and contribute to the improvement of smelter/refiner and upstream due diligence practices, including through any institutionalised mechanism to be established at the industry's initiative, supported by governments and in cooperation with relevant stakeholders.

A. **Plan an independent third party audit of the smelter/refiner's due diligence for responsible supply chains of minerals from conflict-affected and high-risk areas.** The audit should include the following audit scope, criteria, principles and activities:[23]

1. **The scope of the audit:** The audit scope will include all activities, processes and systems used by the smelter/refiner to conduct supply chain due diligence of minerals from conflict-affected and high-risk areas. This includes, but is not limited to, smelter/refiner controls over the mineral supply chain, the information disclosed to downstream companies on suppliers, chain of custody and other mineral information, smelter/refiner risk assessments including the on-the-ground research, and smelter/refiner strategies for risk management.
2. **The audit criteria:** The audit should determine the conformity of the smelter/refiner due diligence process against the standards and processes of this due diligence Guidance.
3. **The audit principles:**
   a) ***Independence:*** To preserve neutrality and impartiality of audits, the audit organisation and all audit team members ("auditors") must be independent from the smelter/refiner as well as from smelter/refiner's subsidiaries, licensees, contractors, suppliers and companies cooperating in the joint audit. This means, in particular, that auditors must not have conflicts of interests with the auditee including business or financial relationship with the auditee (in the form of equity holdings, debt, securities), nor have provided any other services for the auditee company, particularly

23. This recommendation outlines some basic principles, scope, criteria and other basic information for consideration for companies to commission a supply chain-specific independent third-party audit of the due diligence practices of smelters/refiners. Companies should consult ISO International Standard 19011: 2002 ("ISO 19011") for detailed requirements on audit programmes (including programme responsibilities, procedures, record-keeping, monitoring and reviewing) and a step-by-step overview of audit activities.

any services relating to the due diligence practice or the supply chain operations assessed therein, within a 24 month period prior to the audit.[24]

b) ***Competence:*** Auditors should conform to the requirements set out in Chapter 7 of ISO 19011 on Competence and Evaluation of Auditors. Specifically, auditors must have knowledge and skills in the following areas:[25]

i) Auditing principles, procedures and techniques (ISO 19011).

ii) The supply chain due diligence principles, procedures and techniques of the company.

iii) The organisational structure of the company's operations, particularly the company's mineral procurement and mineral supply chain.

iv) The social, cultural and historical contexts of the conflict-affected areas of mineral origin or transport, including relevant linguistic abilities and culturally appropriate sensitivities for conducting audits.

v) All applicable standards, including the model supply chain policy on minerals from conflict-affected and high-risk areas (Annex II).

c) ***Accountability:*** Performance indicators may be used to monitor the ability of the auditors to carry out the audit in conformity with the audit programme, based on the objectives, scope and criteria of the audit, judged against audit programme records.[26]

4. **The audit activities:**

a) ***Audit preparation:*** The objectives, scope, language and criteria for the audit should be clearly communicated to the auditors with any ambiguities clarified between the auditee and auditors before the initiation of the audit.[27] The auditors should determine the feasibility of the audit based on the availability of time, resources, information and cooperation of relevant parties.[28]

b) ***Document review:*** Samples of all documentation produced as part of the smelter/refiner's supply chain due diligence for minerals from conflict affected areas should be reviewed "to determine the conformity of the system, as documented, with audit criteria."[29] This includes, but is not

24. See Chapter VIII (A) of FLA Charter.
25. The requisite knowledge and skill can be determined by the auditor's education and work experience, as laid out in Chapter 7.4 of ISO 19011:2002. Auditors must also exhibit personal attributes of professionalism, impartiality, and honesty.
26. See Chapter 5.6 of ISO 19011.
27. See Chapter 6.2 of ISO 19011.
28. *Ibid.*
29. See 6.3 of ISO 19011.

limited to, documentation on supply chain internal controls (a sample of chain of custody documentation, payment records), relevant communications and contractual provisions with suppliers, documentation generated by company risk assessments (including all records on business partners and suppliers, interviews and on-the-ground assessments), and any documents on risk management strategies (*e.g.* agreements with suppliers on improvement indicators).

c) ***In-site investigations:*** Before beginning the in-site investigations, auditors should prepare an audit plan,[30] and all working documents.[31] The evidence from smelter/refiner supply chain risk assessments and smelter/refiner supply chain risk management should be verified. Auditors should gather further evidence and verify information by conducting relevant interviews, making observations and reviewing documents.[32] In-site investigations should include:

i) **The smelter/refiner facilities** and sites where the smelter/refiner carry out due diligence for responsible supply chains of minerals from conflict-affected and high-risk areas.

ii) **A sample of the smelter/refiner's suppliers** (both international concentrate traders, re-processors and local exporters), which includes supplier facilities.

iii) **A meeting with the assessment team** (*see* Appendix) to review the standards and methods for generating verifiable, reliable and up-to-date information, and audit a sample of evidence relied upon by the smelter/refiner while carrying out due diligence for responsible supply chains of minerals from conflict-affected and high-risk areas. In preparation for the meeting, auditors should request information and submit questions to the on-the-ground assessment team.

iv) **Consultations with local and central governmental authorities, UN expert groups, UN peacekeeping missions and local civil society.**

d) ***Audit Conclusions:*** Auditors should generate findings that determine, based on the evidence gathered, the conformity of the smelter/refiner due diligence for responsible supply chains of minerals from conflict-affected and high-risk areas with this Guidance. Auditors should make recommendations in the audit report for the smelter/refiner to improve their due diligence practices.

30. See 6.4.1 of ISO 19011.
31. See 6.4.3 of ISO 19011.
32. Art. 6.5.4 of ISO 19011.

B. Implement the audit in accordance with the audit scope, criteria, principles and activities set out above.

1. **IMPLEMENTATION OF THE AUDIT.** Under current circumstances, all actors in the supply chain should cooperate through their industry organisations to ensure that the auditing is carried out in accordance with audit scope, criteria, principles and activities listed above.

   a) **SPECIFIC RECOMMENDATIONS – *For local mineral exporters***

      i) Allow access to company sites and all documentation and records of supply chain due diligence.

      ii) Facilitate safe access to on-the-ground assessment team. Coordinate logistics to provide a safe meeting point for audit teams and the on-the-ground assessment team.

   b) **SPECIFIC RECOMMENDATIONS – *For international concentrate traders and mineral re-processors***

      i) Allow access to company sites and all documentation and records of supply chain due diligence.

   c) **SPECIFIC RECOMMENDATIONS – *For smelters/refiners***

      i) Allow access to company sites and all documentation and records of supply chain due diligence.

      ii) Facilitate contact with the sample of suppliers selected by the audit team.

   d) **SPECIFIC RECOMMENDATIONS – *For all downstream companies***

      i) It is recommended that all downstream companies participate and contribute through industry organisations or other suitable means to appoint auditors and define the terms of the audit in line with the standards and processes set out in this Guidance. Small and medium enterprises are encouraged to join or build partnerships with such industry organisations.

2. **INSTITUTIONALISED MECHANISM FOR RESPONSIBLE SUPPLY CHAINS OF MINERALS FROM CONFLICT AFFECTED AND HIGH-RISK AREAS.** All actors in the supply chain, in cooperation and with the support of governments and civil society, may consider incorporating the audit scope, criteria, principles and activities set out above into an institutionalised mechanism that would oversee and support the implementation of due diligence for responsible supply chains of minerals from conflict-affected and high- risk areas. The institution should carry out the following activities:

   a) With regard to audits:

      i) Accrediting auditors;

      ii) Overseeing and verifying audits;

iii) Publishing audit reports with due regard to business confidentiality and competitive concerns.[33]

b) Develop and implement modules to build capabilities of suppliers to conduct due diligence and for suppliers to mitigate risk.

c) Receive and follow-up on grievances of interested parties with the relevant company.

33. See footnote 12.

STEP 5: REPORT ANNUALLY ON SUPPLY CHAIN DUE DILIGENCE

OBJECTIVE: To publicly report on due diligence for responsible supply chains of minerals from conflict-affected and high-risk areas in order to generate public confidence in the measures companies are taking.

A. Annually report or integrate, where practicable, into annual sustainability or corporate responsibility reports, additional information on due diligence for responsible supply chains of minerals from conflict-affected and high-risk areas.

A.1. SPECIFIC RECOMMENDATIONS – *For all upstream companies*

1. *Company Management Systems:* Set out the company's supply chain due diligence policy; explain the management structure responsible for the company's due diligence and who in the company is directly responsible; describe the control systems over the mineral supply chain put in place by the company, explaining how this operates and what data it has yielded that has strengthened the company's due diligence efforts in the reporting period covered; describe the company's database and record-keeping system and explain the methods for disclosing all suppliers, down to the mine of origin, to downstream actors; disclose information on payments made to governments in line with EITI criteria and principles.
2. *Company risk assessment in the supply chain:* Publish the risk assessment with due regard taken of business confidentiality and other competitive concerns.[34] Outline the methodology, practices and information yielded by the on-the-ground assessment; explain the methodology of company supply chain risk assessments.
3. *Risk management:* Describe the steps taken to manage risks, including a summary report on the strategy for risk mitigation in the risk management plan, and capability-training, if any, and the involvement of affected stakeholders. Disclose the efforts made by the company to monitor and track performance.

34. Business confidentiality and other competitive concerns means price information and supplier relationships without prejudice to subsequent evolving interpretation. All information will be disclosed to any institutionalised mechanism, regional or global, once in place with the mandate to collect and process information on minerals from conflict-affected and high-risk areas.

A.2. SPECIFIC RECOMMENDATIONS – *For smelters/refiners*

1. *Audits:* Publish the audit reports of smelters/refiners with due regard taken of business confidentiality and other competitive concerns.[35]

A.3. SPECIFIC RECOMMENDATIONS – *For all downstream companies*

1. *Company Management Systems:* Set out the company's supply chain due diligence policy; explain the management structure responsible for the company's due diligence and who in the company is directly responsible.
2. *Risk assessment and management:* Describe the steps taken to identify smelters/refiners in the supply chain and assess their due diligence practices, including the published list of qualified smelters/refiners through industry validation schemes conforming to the due diligence processes recommended in this Guidance. Describe the steps taken to manage risks.
3. *Audits:* Publish the audit reports of their due diligence practices, with due regard taken of business confidentiality and other competitive concerns[36] and responses to identified risks.

35. See footnote 34.
36. See footnote 34.

APPENDIX

Guiding Note for Upstream Company Risk Assessment

A. Create enabling conditions for an effective risk assessment.

When planning and structuring the supply chain risk assessment, upstream companies in the supply chain should take into account the following recommended actions:

1. ***Use an evidence-based approach.*** Conclusions of the company risk assessment should be corroborated by verifiable, reliable, up-to-date evidence, which should be gained through on-the-ground research carried out by an on-the ground assessment team.
2. ***Preserve the reliability and quality of company fact and risk assessment of a supply chain***, by ensuring that company assessors are independent from the activity being assessed and free from conflict of interests.[37] Company assessors must commit to reporting truthfully and accurately and upholding the highest professional ethical standards and exercise "due professional care".[38]
3. ***Ensure the appropriate level of competence***, by employing experts with knowledge and skill in as many of the following areas: the operational contexts assessed (*e.g.* linguistic abilities, cultural sensitivities), the substance of conflict-related risks (*e.g.* the standards in Annex II, human rights, international humanitarian law, corruption, financial crime, conflict and financing parties to a conflict, transparency), the nature and form of the mineral supply chain (*e.g.* mineral procurement), and the standards and process contained in this due diligence Guidance.

B. Establish an on-the-ground assessment team (hereafter "assessment team") in the conflict-affected and high-risk

37. Art. 4, ISO 19011:2002
38. Art. 4, ISO 19011:2002

areas of mineral origin and transit to generate and maintain information on suppliers and the circumstances of mineral extraction, trade, handling and export. Upstream companies may establish such a team jointly in cooperation with other upstream companies supplying from, or operating in these areas ("cooperating companies").

1. Upstream companies establishing the assessment team should:

   a) Ensure the assessment team consults with local and central governments to gain information, with a view to strengthening cooperation and opening avenues of communication between government institutions, civil society and local suppliers.

   b) Ensure the assessment team regularly consults with local civil society organisations with local knowledge and expertise.

   c) Establish or support the creation, where appropriate, of community-monitoring networks to feed information into the assessment team.

   d) Share information gained and maintained by the assessment team throughout the entire supply chain, preferably through a computerized system with web accessibility for companies in the supply chain and any institutionalised mechanism, regional or global, once in place with the mandate to collect and process information on minerals from conflict-affected and high-risk areas.

2. Upstream companies establishing the assessment team should define the scope and capacities of the on-the-ground assessment team to undertake the following activities:

   a) Obtain first-hand evidence of the factual circumstances of mineral extraction, trade, handling and export. This includes:

      i) **The militarisation of mine sites, transportation routes and points where minerals are traded.** The assessment team should track the militarisation of mine sites, transportation routes and points where minerals are traded. Interactive maps which indicate the location of mines, armed groups, trade routes, roadblocks and airfields can constitute an additional source of information for companies.[39] Tracking the militarisation of mines, transportation routes and points where minerals are traded means identifying factual circumstances resulting in direct or indirect support to non-state armed groups and public or private security forces (as defined in the model supply chain policy in Annex II).

      ii) **Serious abuses associated with the extraction, transport or trade of minerals (as defined in the model supply chain policy in Annex II)**

39. Such as DRC Map, US Department of State Map, IPIS map.

committed by public or private security forces, non-state armed groups or other third parties operating in mining areas, along transportation routes or points where minerals are traded.

b) Respond to specific questions or requests for clarifications made by cooperating companies and put forward recommendations for the company risk assessment and risk management. All cooperating companies may put forward questions to, or request clarifications from, the on-the-ground assessment team on the following:[40]

i) Evidence generated by the traceability and chain of custody system [Step 1 (C)] and the risk assessment [Step 2].

ii) Information on suppliers (intermediaries and exporters) in line with "Know your customer/supplier" protocols, such as those implemented through anti-money laundering compliance systems.[41]

c) Receive and assess grievances voiced by interested parties on the ground and communicate to cooperating companies.

B.1. *SPECIFIC RECOMMENDATIONS – For local exporters*

1. Facilitate local logistics for the assessment team, responding to any requests for assistance.
2. Facilitate assessment team's access to all upstream intermediaries, consolidators and transporters.
3. Allow the assessment team access to all company sites, including in neighbouring countries or other countries where trans-shipment or relabeling is likely, as well as all books, records or other evidence of procurement practices, tax, fee and royalty payments, and export documentation.
4. Allow the assessment team access to all information gained and maintained as part of the company's due diligence practices, including payments made to non-state armed groups and public or private security forces.
5. Identify relevant personnel to act as contact points for the assessment team.

40. Questions and clarifications should be recorded and feed into information systems for future use, monitoring and updating, jointly accessible by cooperating companies.
41. See, Financial Action Task Force, Guidance on the risk-based approach to combating money laundering and terrorist financing, June 2007, Section 3.10.

B.2. SPECIFIC RECOMMENDATIONS – *For international concentrate traders and mineral re-processors*

1. Facilitate assessment team's access to all cross-border transporters, allowing them to join cross-border transportation of minerals on an unannounced basis.
2. Allow assessment teams access to all sites owned by the international concentrate traders and mineral re-processors in neighbouring countries or other countries where trans-shipment or relabeling is likely for minerals from conflict-affected and high-risk areas or where leakages in the supply chain are known or likely to exist.
3. Allow assessment team access to all books, records or other evidence of procurement practices, tax, fee and royalty payments, and export documentation.
4. Allow the assessment team access to all information gained and maintained as part of the company's due diligence practices, including payments made to non-state armed groups and public or private security forces.
5. Proactively provide assessment team with records of minerals from other red flag locations of mineral origin and transit.
6. Identify relevant personnel to act as contact points for the assessment team.

B.3. SPECIFIC RECOMMENDATIONS – *For smelters/refiners*

1. Identify relevant personnel to act as contact points for the assessment team.
2. Allow assessment team access to all books, records or other evidence of procurement practices, tax, fee and royalty payments, and export documentation.
3. Allow the assessment team access to all information gained and maintained as part of the company's due diligence practices.

C. RECOMMENDED QUESTIONS THAT COMPANY ASSESSMENTS SHOULD ANSWER: These questions relate to common circumstances found in the supply chain of tin, tantalum, tungsten, their ores and metal derivates which give rise to risks.

1. **Know the context of the conflict-affected and high-risk area of mineral origin, transit and/or export**

   a) Study profiles on the conflict-affected and high-risk areas of origin, neighbouring and transit countries (including potential transportation routes and the locations of extraction, trade, handling, and export). Relevant information will include public reports (from governments, international organisations, NGOs, and media), maps, UN reports and UN Security Council sanctions, industry literature relating to mineral extraction, and its impact on conflict, human rights or environmental harm in the country of potential origin, or other public statements (*e.g.* from ethical pension funds).

b) Are there international entities capable of intervention and investigation, such as UN peacekeeping units, based in or near the area? Can these systems be used to identify actors in the supply chain? Are there local means for recourse to address concerns related to the presence of armed groups or other elements of conflict? Are relevant national, provincial, and/or local regulatory agencies with jurisdiction over mining issues capable of addressing such concerns?

2. **Know your suppliers and business partners**[42]

a) Who are the suppliers or other parties involved in financing, extracting, trading and transporting the minerals between point of extraction and the point at which the company undertaking the due diligence takes custody of the minerals? Identify all significant actors in the supply chain, collecting information on ownership (including beneficial ownership), corporate structure, the names of corporate officers and directors, the ownership interests of the company or officers in other organisations, the business, government, political or military affiliations of the company and officers (in particular, focusing on potential relationships with non-state armed groups or public or private security forces).[43]

b) What procurement and due diligence systems do these suppliers have in place? What supply chain policies have suppliers adopted and how have they integrated them into their management processes? How do they establish internal controls over minerals? How do they enforce policies and conditions on their suppliers?

3. **Know the conditions of mineral extraction in conflict affected and high-risk areas**

a) What is the exact origin of the minerals (what are the specific mines)?

b) What was the method of extraction? Identify if minerals were extracted through artisanal and small-scale mining ("ASM") or large-scale mining,

42. See Financial Action Task Force, Guidance on the risk-based approach to combating money laundering and terrorist financing, June 2007, Section 3.10. See Step 2.
43. See Chapter VI of *Guidelines on reputational due diligence*, International Association of Oil and Gas Producers (Report No. 356, 2004). See also Chapter 5 "Knowing Clients and Business Partners" of the *OECD Risk Awareness Tool for Multinational Enterprises in Weak Governance Zones*, 2006.

and if through ASM, identify, where possible, whether extracted by individual artisanal miners, artisanal mining cooperatives, associations, or small enterprises. Identify the taxes, royalties and fees paid to government institutions, and the disclosures made on those payments.

c) Do conditions of extraction involve the presence and involvement of non-state armed groups or public or private security forces, including in one or more of the following: direct control of the mine or transportation routes around mine; levying of taxes on miners or extortion of minerals; beneficial or other ownership interests in the mine site or mineral rights by non-state armed groups or public or private security forces and/or their families and/or associates; engagement in mining as a second income when "off duty"; or provision of security paid by miners or through taxes arising from production. Do any of these armed groups or military units have an involvement or interest in the conflict? Do any of them have a history of involvement in widespread human rights abuses or other crimes?

d) What are the conditions of extraction? In particular, identify if there are *i)* any forms of torture, cruel, inhuman and degrading treatment exacted for the purposes of mineral extraction; *ii)* any forms of forced or compulsory labour which means work or service which is exacted from any person under the menace of penalty and for which said person has not offered himself voluntarily; *iii)* the worst forms of child labour for the purposes of mineral extraction; *iv)* other gross human rights violations and abuses such as widespread sexual violence on mine sites or in the course of mineral extraction; or *v)* war crimes or other serious violations of international humanitarian law, crimes against humanity or genocide.

4. **Know the conditions of mineral transport, handling and trade in conflict affected and high-risk areas**

a) Were downstream purchasers situated at the mine site or elsewhere? Were the minerals from different miners handled and processed separately and kept separate when sold downstream? If not, at what point were the minerals processed, consolidated and mixed when sold downstream?

b) Who were the intermediaries that handled the minerals? Identify whether any of those intermediaries have been reported or suspected to be extracting or trading minerals associated with non-state armed groups.

c) To what extent, if any, are public or private security forcesor non-state armed groups directly or indirectly involved in the trading, transportation or taxing of the minerals? Are the public or private security forces or non-state armed groups benefiting in any way from the trading, transportating or taxing of minerals being carried out by other parties, including through affiliations with intermediaries or exporters?

d) To what extent, if any, are the public or private security forces or non-state armed groups present along trade and transportation routes? Are there any human rights abuses occurring in trading, transportation or taxing of the minerals? For example, is there evidence of forced labour, extortion or coercion being used? Is child labour being used? In particular, identify if there are *i)* any forms of torture, cruel, inhuman and degrading treatment exacted for the purposes of mineral transport or trade; *ii)* any forms of forced or compulsory labour to mine, transport, trade or sell minerals; *iii)* the worst forms of child labour for the purposes of mineral transport or trade; *iv)* other gross human rights violations and abuses such as widespread sexual violence on mine sites or in the course of mineral transport or trade; or *v)* war crimes or other serious violations of international humanitarian law, crimes against humanity or genocide for the purposes of mineral transport or trade.

e) What information is available to verify the downstream trade, such as authentic documents, transportation routes, licensing, cross-border transportation, and the presence of armed groups and/or public or private security forces?

5. **Know the conditions of export from conflict affected and high-risk areas**

a) What was the point of export and have there been reports or are there suspicions of facilitation payments or other bribes paid at points of export to conceal or fraudulently misrepresent the mineral origin? What documents accompanied mineral export and have there been reports or are there suspicions of fraudulent documentation or inaccurately described declarations (on type of mineral, mineral quality, origin, weight, etc.)? What taxes, duties or other fees were paid on export and have there been reports or are there suspicions of under-declaration?

b) How was export transportation coordinated and how was it carried out? Who are the transporters and have there been reports or are there suspicions of their engagement in corruption (facilitation payment, bribes, under-declarations, etc.)? How was export financing and insurance obtained?

© OECD 2016

Supplement on Gold

Introduction and scope

This *Supplement on Gold* forms an integral part of the OECD *Due Diligence Guidance for Minerals from Conflict-Affected and High-Risk Areas*. The Introductory section of the Guidance as well as Annex I (*Five-Step Framework for Risk-Based Due Diligence in the Mineral Supply Chain*), Annex II (*Model Supply Chain Policy for a Responsible Global Supply Chain of Minerals from Conflict-Affected and High-Risk Areas*) and Annex III (*Suggested Measures for Risk Mitigation and Indicators for Measuring Improvement*) applies to the Supplement on Gold. Therefore the term "Guidance" may be used throughout this Supplement to refer to both this Supplement on Gold as well as the *OECD Due Diligence Guidance for Minerals from Conflict-Affected and High-Risk Areas*.

This Supplement provides specific guidance on supply chain due diligence of gold from conflict-affected and high-risk areas according to the different positions of companies in the gold supply chain. It distinguishes between the roles of and the corresponding due diligence recommendations addressed to *upstream companies* and *downstream companies* in the supply chain (see Definitions), and includes, where necessary, specific recommendations to the specific actors within those two broad categories. Companies falling into these categories should carry out due diligence regardless of whether they own, lease or loan the gold.

This Supplement focuses on the steps companies should take to avoid contributing to conflict and serious abuses of human rights in the supply chain of gold potentially sourced from conflict-affected and high-risk areas. This Supplement includes due diligence measures to be taken on recycled/scrap or previously refined gold ("Recyclable Gold") only insofar as recycled material is a potential means of laundering gold that has been mined in conflict-affected and high-risk areas in order to hide its origin. Gold investment products (ingots, bars, coins, and grain in sealed containers) held in bullion bank vaults, central bank vaults, exchanges and refineries with a "verifiable date"[1] prior to 1 January 2012 will not require information on their origin ("Grandfathered Stocks"). However, gold investment products will require "Know Your Counterparty" due diligence to ensure the trade in Grandfathered stocks is not carried out in violation of international sanctions

1. "Verifiable date" is date which can be verified through inspection of physical date stamps on products as well as inventory lists. See definitions.

or does not enable money-laundering resulting from, or connected to, the sale of gold reserves in conflict-affected and high-risk areas.

In order to determine the applicability of this Supplement, all companies in the gold supply chain should carry out Step 1 (Establish strong company management systems) and begin Step 2 (Identify and assess risks in the supply chain) to determine whether they actually or potentially source gold from conflict-affected and high-risk areas. The remainder of the Steps in this Supplement will then only apply to companies sourcing gold from conflict-affected and high-risk areas and actors in the gold supply chain that operate in a conflict-affected or high-risk area.

In addition to providing the principles, standards and processes for the performance of due diligence by individual companies, the Guidance and this Supplement recommends due diligence principles, standards and processes that emerging industry-wide supply chain initiatives should meet as they work towards conflict-sensitive responsible sourcing practices. The development of comprehensive certification schemes, such as the International Conference of the Great Lakes Region certification scheme and tools, or other industry or multi-stakeholder initiatives that provide for verification processes of conflict-free gold sourcing practices consistent with the standards and processes contained in this Guidance may deliver credible assurance that a supply chain does not contribute to conflict or serious human rights abuses.[2]

This Guidance recognises that due diligence in conflict-affected and high- risk areas presents practical challenges. Flexibility is needed in the application of due diligence. The nature and extent of due diligence that is appropriate will depend on individual circumstances and be affected by factors such as the size of the enterprise, the location of the activities, the situation in a particular country, the sector and nature of the products or services involved. These challenges may be met in a variety of ways, including but not limited to:

- Industry-wide cooperation in building capacity to conduct due diligence.
- Cost-sharing within industry for specific due diligence tasks.
- Participation in initiatives on responsible supply chain management.[3]

2. See definition of contributing to conflict in Annex II of OECD Guidance.
3. For example provided they are consistent with the OECD Guidance: *Conflict-Free Smelter Program*; *Conflict Free Gold Standard*, World Gold Council (2012); *Responsible Gold Guidance*, London Bullion Market Association (2012); and *Chain-of-Custody Certification*, Responsible Jewellery Council (2012); *Fairtrade and Fairmined Standard for Gold from Artisanal and Small-Scale Mining*, Alliance of Responsible Mining/ Fairtrade Labelling Organizations International (2010).

- Coordination between industry members who share suppliers.
- Cooperation between upstream and downstream companies.
- Building partnerships with international and civil society organisations.
- Integrating the model supply chain policy (Annex II) and specific due diligence recommendations outlined in this Guidance into existing policies and management systems, due diligence practices of the company, such as procurement practices, integrity and know your customer due diligence measures and sustainability, corporate social responsibility or other annual reporting.

The Guidance in particular recognises that due diligence regarding artisanal and small-scale gold mining in conflict-affected and high-risk areas presents challenges. Artisanal and small-scale gold producers such as individuals, informal working groups or communities are not expected to carry out due diligence as recommended in this Guidance, but they are encouraged to remain involved in due diligence efforts of their customers and formalise so they can carry out due diligence in the future. Only artisanal and small-scale enterprises are expected to carry out due diligence (see Definitions). Suggested measures are contained in the Appendix to prevent potentially harmful social and economic impacts on vulnerable groups[4] in conflict-affected and high-risk areas, including legitimate artisanal and small-scale miners.

Given the complex operating environments of conflict-affected and high-risk areas, where conditions can evolve and degenerate rapidly, due diligence is understood as an on-going proactive and reactive process whereby companies take reasonable steps and make good faith efforts to identify and respond to risks of contributing to conflict and serious abuses in accordance with this Guidance, and in particular Annex II. This Guidance promotes progressive improvement to due diligence practices through constructive engagement with suppliers. Companies are encouraged to integrate this Guidance into their broader policies and practices on responsible business conduct, and are encouraged to inform consumers and the public at large that they are implementing this Guidance. Companies may use this Guidance to

4. *See* OECD Guidelines for Multinational Enterprises (2011), Commentary on Chapter IV Human Rights, paragraph 40: "[...] enterprises should respect the human rights of individuals belonging to specific groups or populations that require particular attention, where they may have adverse human rights impacts on them. In this connection, United Nations instruments have elaborated further on the rights of indigenous peoples; persons belonging to national or ethnic, religious and linguistic minorities; women; children; persons with disabilities; and migrant workers and their families."

make reasonable determinations as to the responsible conflict-sensitive nature of their products.

This Guidance builds on and is consistent with the principles and standards contained in the OECD Guidelines for Multinational Enterprises and the OECD Risk Awareness Tool for Multinational Enterprises in Weak Governance Zones. It provides recommendations jointly addressed by governments to companies operating in or sourcing minerals from conflict-affected and high-risk areas, providing guidance on principles and due diligence processes for responsible supply chains of minerals from conflict-affected and high-risk areas, consistent with applicable laws and relevant internationally recognised standards. As such, this Guidance is not a substitute for nor should it be considered to override domestic laws and regulations, including those relating to mining.[5]

Definitions

Artisanal and Small-scale Mining (ASM) – formal or informal mining operations with predominantly simplified forms of exploration, extraction, processing, and transportation. ASM is normally low capital intensive and uses high labour intensive technology. "ASM" can include men and women working on an individual basis as well as those working in family groups, in partnership, or as members of cooperatives or other types of legal associations and enterprises involving hundreds or even thousands of miners. For example, it is common for work groups of 4-10 individuals, sometimes in family units, to share tasks at one single point of mineral extraction (*e.g.* excavating one tunnel). At the organisational level, groups of 30-300 miners are common, extracting jointly one mineral deposit (*e.g.* working in different tunnels), and sometimes sharing processing facilities.[6]

ASM Enterprises – Artisanal and small-scale entities that are sufficiently formalised and structured to carry out this Guidance. As per the Appendix, all artisanal and small-scale miners are encouraged to formalise in this regard.

Bullion – The generic word for refined gold in bar or ingot form.

Bullion bank – A bank (including retail, commercial and investment banks) or financial institution such as a trading house, that conducts financial transactions in refined gold.

Chain of custody – A record of the sequence of entities which have custody of minerals as they move through a supply chain.

5. See Chapter I, paragraph 2, OECD Guidelines for Multinational Enterprises (2011).
6. *See* Felix Hruschka and Cristina Echavarría, Rock-Solid Chances for Responsible Artisanal Mining, Alliance for Responsible Mining Series on Responsible ASM No.3, 2011.

Conflict-affected and high-risk areas – Areas identified by the presence of armed conflict, widespread violence, including violence generated by criminal networks, or other risks of serious and widespread harm to people. Armed conflict may take a variety of forms, such as a conflict of international or non-international character, which may involve two or more states, or may consist of wars of liberation, or insurgencies, civil wars. *High-risk areas* are those where there is a high risk of conflict or of widespread or serious abuses as defined in paragraph 1 of Annex II of the Guidance. Such areas are often characterised by political instability or repression, institutional weakness, insecurity, collapse of civil infrastructure, widespread violence and violations of national or international law.

"Direct or indirect support" to non-state armed groups or public or private security forces through the extraction, transport, trade, handling or export of gold includes, but is not limited to, procuring minerals from, making payments to or otherwise providing logistical assistance or equipment to, non-state armed groups or their affiliates who:[7]

i) illegally control mine sites or otherwise control transportation routes, points where gold is traded and upstream actors in the supply chain;[8] and/or

ii) illegally tax or extort[9] money or gold at points of access to mine sites, along transportation routes or at points where gold is traded; and/or

iii) illegally tax or extort intermediaries, export companies or international traders.

Due diligence – Due diligence is an on-going, proactive and reactive process through which companies can identify, prevent, mitigate and account for how they address their actual and potential adverse impacts as an integral part of business decision-making and risk management systems. Due diligence can help companies ensure they observe the principles of

7. "Affiliates" includes négociants, consolidators, intermediaries, and others in the supply chain that work directly with armed groups to facilitate the extraction, trade or handling of gold.
8. "Control" of mines, transportation routes, points where gold is traded and upstream actors in the supply chain means *i)* overseeing extraction, including by granting access to mine sites and/or coordinating downstream sales to intermediaries, export companies or international traders; *ii)* making recourse to any forms of forced or compulsory labour to mine, transport, trade or sell gold; or *iii)* acting as a director or officer of, or holding beneficial or other ownership interests in, upstream companies or mines.
9. "Extort" from mines, transportation routes, points where gold is traded or upstream companies means the demanding, under the threat of violence or any other penalty, and for which the person has not voluntarily offered, sums of money or gold, often in return for granting access to exploit the mine site, access transportation routes, or to transport, purchase, or sell gold.

GOLD SOURCES

For the purpose of this Guidance, there are three possible sources of gold and gold-bearing material, for which different due diligence is recommended:

1) MINED GOLD – Gold that originates from mines (medium and large-scale or artisanal and/or small-scale mines) and has never been previously refined. The *origin* of Mined Gold is the mine where it was extracted. Sub-categories of mined gold before it is refined are:

- **Alluvial gold** – Newly mined gold that has been taken from sand and gravel deposits, most often in or near streams, typically as very small but visible pieces of gold. Alluvial gold is usually in the form of "dust," occasionally nuggets, which is already concentrated in form, easily transported, and may be easily melted and/or semi-refined into small ingots (normally of 85% – 92 % purity). Alluvial gold in all of these forms requires refining before use as bullion or jewellery, but can ordinarily be directly refined, without further intermediate concentration or processing.
- **Gold ore** – Rock or gravel that contains an economically valuable concentration of gold. This concentration may be very small by weight, *e.g.*, 1 gram of gold per tonne of ore, and still be economically recoverable in medium and large-scale industrial mining. Gold ore, because of its bulk and weight, is ordinarily not transported far from a mine site for processing.
- **Gold concentrate** – An intermediate material produced from processing of gold ore to achieve a higher concentration, but still requiring further intermediate processing to produce doré. A gold concentrate would ordinarily be transported to a nearby gold smelter for creation of doré.
- **Gold doré** – A bar of newly mined gold metal alloy, generally originating from extensive processing of ores and smelting at medium and large-scale mines to a high concentration (normally of 85% – 90% purity). Mined gold in this form is not commercial quality and must then be transported to a refinery to be directly refined, without further intermediate processing.
- **Mining Byproduct** – Gold that is produced from other metal mining, *e.g.*, from copper sulphide ore, in which gold may be a trace constituent. When gold is a byproduct, the other more important metal is processed and refined first, and the gold is then extracted and refined from the final residue of the first metal, such as a copper electrolytic cell slime.
- **LSM Gold** – Gold that has been produced by Medium and Large-scale Mining (see Definition of Medium and Large-scale Mining).
- **ASM Gold** – Gold that has been produced by Artisanal and Small-scale Mining (see Definition of Artisanal and Small-scale Mining).

GOLD SOURCES *(cont.)*

2) RECYCLABLE GOLD – Gold that has been previously refined, such as end-user, post-consumer and investment gold and gold-bearing products, and scrap and waste metals and materials arising during refining and product manufacturing, which is returned to a refiner or other downstream intermediate processor to begin a new life cycle as 'recycled gold'. The *origin* of Recyclable Gold is considered to be the point in the gold supply chain where the gold is returned to the refiner or other downstream intermediate processor or recycler. Sub-categories of recyclable gold are:

- **Unprocessed recyclable gold** – Recyclable Gold still in its original form and/or fabrication scrap, before it has been returned for processing and refining (*e.g.* bullion bars, pieces of jewellery, ornaments, coins, machine turnings, etc.)
- **Melted recyclable gold** – Recyclable Gold which has been melted as the first recycling process and cast into rudimentary bars or some other form with undefined dimensions and variable fineness.
- **Industrial By-product** – A material produced while processing another material, not the primary intended product but nevertheless a separate useful material. For example, gold refining often creates low value by-products such as furnace flue dust, spent crucibles and floor sweepings.

3) GRANDFATHERED STOCKS – Gold investment products (ingots, bars, coins, and grain in sealed containers) held in bullion bank vaults, central bank vaults, exchanges and refineries with a verifiable date prior to 1 January 2012, which will not require a determination of origin. This includes stocks held by a third party on behalf of the listed entities.

- **Verifiable Date:** A date which can be verified through inspection of physical date stamps on products and/or inventory lists.

Mixed Gold – Gold that includes multiple sources (*e.g.*, both mined gold and recyclable gold). Due diligence should be conducted on those sources of mixed gold in accordance with the recommendations in this Supplement

international law and comply with domestic laws, including those governing the illicit trade in minerals and United Nations sanctions.

Good Delivery – A standard of physical specifications for refined gold and for capabilities of gold refiners that is accepted on an exchange or in an over-the-counter ("OTC") market (*e.g.* London Good Delivery).

Industry Programme – For the purpose of this Guidance, this term means an initiative or programme created and managed by an industry organisation or similar industry initiative to support and advance some or all of the recommendations of this Guidance. An Industry Programme may be a part of the organisation's broader activities that encompass other goals. Any reference in this Guidance to relevant activities and/or initiatives of an

Industry Programme is understood to mean that such activities and/or initiatives will be consistent with this Guidance.

Institutionalised Mechanism – For the purpose of this Guidance, this term means an organisation created by and composed of representatives of governments, industries and civil society with a mandate to support and advance some or all of the recommendations of this Guidance. Any reference in this Guidance to relevant activities and/or initiatives of an Institutionalised Mechanism is understood to mean that such activities and/or initiatives will be consistent with this Guidance.

Legitimate artisanal and small-scale mining: The legitimacy of artisanal and small-scale mining is a difficult concept to define because it involves a number of situation-specific factors (see Appendix). For the purposes of this Guidance, legitimate refers, *among others,* to artisanal and small-scale mining that is consistent with applicable laws.[10] When the applicable legal framework is not enforced, or in the absence of such a framework, the assessment of the legitimacy of artisanal and small-scale mining will take into account the good faith efforts of artisanal and small-scale miners and enterprises to operate within the applicable legal framework (where it exists) as well as their engagement in opportunities for formalisation as they become available (bearing in mind that in most cases, artisanal and small-scale miners have very limited or no capacity, technical ability or sufficient financial resources to do so). In either case, Artisanal and small-scale mining, as with all mining, cannot be considered legitimate when it contributes to conflict and serious abuses associated with the extraction, transport or trade of minerals as defined in Annex II of the Guidance.

Management system – Management processes and documentation that collectively provide a systematic framework for ensuring that tasks are performed correctly, consistently and effectively to achieve the desired outcomes, and that provide for continual improvement in performance.

Medium and Large-Scale Mining (LSM) – For the purposes of this Guidance, LSM refers to gold mining operations that are not considered to be artisanal or small-scale mining.

Recycler – an individual or entity that is not a refiner as defined below, that collects, consolidates and/or processes recyclable/scrap gold, such as sampling and assay, prior to refining to begin a new life cycle.

10. See *Vision for Responsible Artisanal and Small-scale Mining in Alliance for Responsible Mining* (Echavarria, C. *et. al.* Eds.), (2008) The Golden Vein – A guide to responsible artisanal and small-scale mining. ARM Series on Responsible ASM No. 1. Medellin.

Refiner – an individual or entity that purifies gold to a commercial market quality, by removing other substances from doré, alluvial gold, recyclable/ scrap or other gold-bearing feedstocks.

Suppliers – This term refers to any individual or organisation who is considered to be a participant in the supply chain for the supply of gold and gold-bearing materials.

Supply chain – The term supply chain refers to the system of all the activities, organisations, actors, technology, information, resources and services involved in moving gold from the source to end consumers.

Upstream supply chain and Upstream Companies – "Upstream supply chain" means the gold supply chain from the mine to refiners. "Upstream companies" include miners (artisanal and small-scale enterprises or medium and large-scale gold mining companies),[11] local gold traders or exporters from the country of gold origin, transporters, international gold traders of Mined/Recyclable Gold and refiners. Artisanal and small-scale gold producers such as individuals, informal working groups or communities are not expected included as upstream companies for the purposes of carrying out due diligence in line with this Guidance, although they are encouraged to remain involved in due diligence efforts of their customers and formalise so they can carry out due diligence in the future.

Downstreamsupply chain and Downstream Companies – "Downstream supply chain" means the gold supply chain from refiners to retailers. "Downstream companies" include refined gold traders and gold markets, bullion banks and exchanges or other entities that do their own gold vaulting, jewellery manufacturers and retailers, and other companies using gold in the fabrication of products (*e.g.* manufacturers and retailers of electronics or medical devices).

Supply Chain Due Diligence: With specific regard to supply chain due diligence for responsible mineral sourcing, risk-based due diligence refers to the steps companies should take to identify, prevent and mitigate actual and potential adverse impacts and ensure that they respect human rights and do not contribute to conflict[12] through their activities in the supply chain.[13]

11. For the avoidance of doubt, these guidelines include miners, processors and refiners which may be owned or otherwise controlled or directed by governments or other State entities.
12. As defined in Annex II of the OECD Due Diligence Guidance.
13. OECD Guidelines for Multinational Enterprises (OECD, 2011); OECD Risk Awareness Tool for Multinational Enterprises in Weak Governance Zones, (OECD, 2006); Guiding Principles on Business and Human Rights: Implementing the United Nations "Protect, Respect and Remedy" Framework, 21 March 2011 (A/HRC/17/31).

Figure 2. **Risks in the supply chain of gold from conflict-affected and high-risk areas**

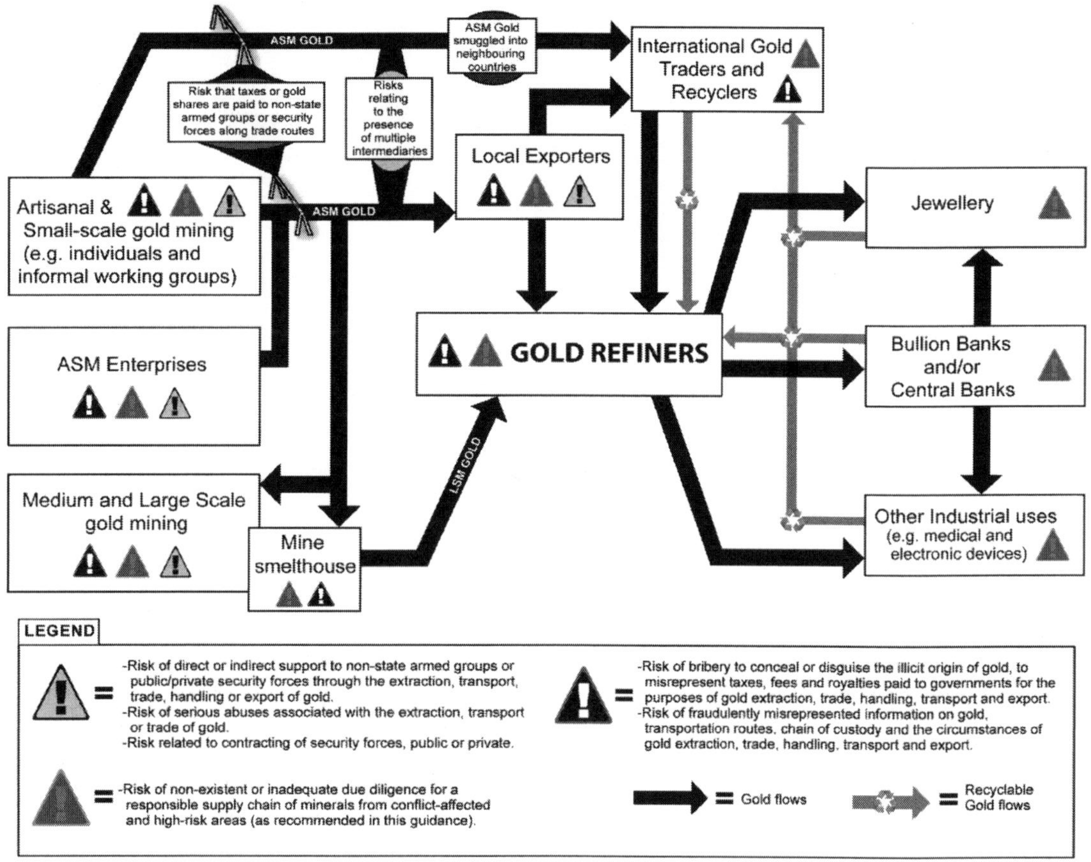

STEP 1: ESTABLISH STRONG COMPANY MANAGEMENT SYSTEMS

OBJECTIVE: To ensure that existing due diligence and management systems of companies in the gold supply chain are structured for effective due diligence.

SECTION I – GENERAL RECOMMENDATIONS FOR ALL COMPANIES IN THE GOLD SUPPLY CHAIN

A. Adopt and commit to a supply chain policy for identifying and managing risks for gold potentially from conflict-affected and high-risk areas.
This policy, for all companies in the supply chain, should include:

1. A policy commitment setting forth common principles and standards for responsible supply chains of gold from conflict-affected and high-risk areas, against which the company will assess itself and the activities and relationships of suppliers. This policy should be consistent with the standards set forth in the model supply chain policy in Annex II of the Guidance.
2. A clear and coherent management process to ensure risks are adequately managed. The company should commit to the due diligence steps and recommendations outlined for the various levels identified in this Supplement.

B. Structure internal management systems to support supply chain due diligence.
Companies in the supply chain should:

1. Assign authority and responsibility to senior staff with the necessary competence, knowledge and experience to oversee the supply chain due diligence process.
2. Ensure availability of resources necessary to support the operation and monitoring of these processes.
3. Put in place an organisational structure and communication processes that will ensure critical information, including the company policy, reaches relevant employees and suppliers. Training as appropriate should be carried out, and companies may consider training modules developed by Industry Programmes or Institutionalised Mechanisms.
4. Ensure internal accountability with respect to the implementation of the supply chain due diligence process.

C. Establish a system of transparency, information collection and control over the gold supply chain.

1. Create internal documentation and records of supply chain due diligence processes, findings and resulting decisions. This will include Step 1 due diligence, as well as additional due diligence that may be carried out with regard to gold supply chains from conflict-affected and high-risk areas (Steps 2-5).
2. Maintain internal inventory and transaction documentation that can be retrieved and used to retrospectively identify gold inputs and outputs and/or support a chain-of-custody system (see Step 3 (B)). This should include:
   a) Information regarding the form, type and physical description of gold and gold-bearing materials, *e.g.* gold ore, gold concentrate, gold doré, alluvial gold, recyclable gold, gold bullion, jewellery manufacturing inputs and/or products, electronic components and gold plating solutions, etc. (see "Definitions" section of this Supplement).

   b) Information provided by the supplier regarding the weight and assay of gold and gold-bearing materials of input, and determinations of the weight and assay of gold inputs and outputs.

   c) Supplier details, including "know your counterparty" ("KYC") due diligence information consistent with the 40 Recommendations of the Financial Action Task Force (FATF).[14]

   d) Unique reference numbers for each input and output.

   e) Dates of input and output, purchases and sales.
3. Make and receive payments for gold through official banking channels where they are reasonably available. Avoid cash purchases where possible, and ensure that all unavoidable cash purchases are supported by verifiable documentation.
4. Cooperate fully and transparently with law enforcement agencies regarding gold transactions. Provide customs officials with access to complete information regarding all shipments that cross international borders, or to which they otherwise have jurisdiction.
5. Maintain the information collected above for a minimum of five years, preferably on a computerised database.

D. Strengthen company engagement with suppliers. Companies in the supply chain should seek to influence their suppliers to commit to a

14. See Financial Acton Task Force (FATF) 40 Recommendations (2003). See also Financial Action Task Force, *RBA Guidance for Dealers in Precious Metal and Stones* (2008).

supply chain policy consistent with Annex II and the due diligence processes in this Guidance. In order to do this, the company should:

1. Aim to establish long-term relationships with suppliers in order to build responsible sourcing relationships with them.
2. Communicate to suppliers the expectations on due diligence for responsible supply chains of gold from conflict-affected and high-risk areas, consistent with Annex II of the Guidance and this Supplement. In particular, companies should communicate their expectation that their suppliers should determine a risk management strategy with respect to identified risks in the supply chain, consistent with Annex II of the Guidance.
3. Incorporate the supply chain policy set out in this Guidance into commercial contracts and/or written agreements with suppliers which can be applied and monitored.[15]
4. Consider ways to support and build capabilities of suppliers to improve performance and conform to company supply chain policy.[16]
5. Commit to risk management, which may include designing measurable improvement plans with suppliers with the involvement, if relevant and where appropriate, of local and central governments, international organisations and civil society when pursuing risk mitigation.[17]

E. Establish a company and/or mine level grievance mechanism.

Depending on their position in the supply chain companies should:

1. Develop an early warning risk awareness mechanism allowing any interested party (affected persons or whistle-blowers) to voice concerns regarding the circumstances of gold extraction, trade, handling and export in a conflict-affected or high-risk area. This will allow a company to be alerted of risks in its supply chain in addition to the company's own fact and risk assessments.
2. Provide such a mechanism directly, or through collaborative arrangements with other companies or organisations such as an Industry Programme or Institutionalised Mechanism, or by facilitating recourse to an external expert or body (*i.e.* ombudsman).

15. See Steps 2-5 for information on monitoring suppliers and managing non-compliance.
16. See Step 3, "Risk Mitigation".
17. See step 3, "Risk Mitigation".

SECTION II – SPECIFIC RECOMMENDATIONS

A. For medium and large-scale gold mining companies and artisanal and small-scale mining enterprises:

1. Assign a unique reference number to each output, *e.g.* bar of gold doré, or container of alluvial gold, and affix and/or imprint that reference number in such a manner that its tampering or removal will be evident.
2. Adopt physical security practices over gold such as sealed security boxes for shipment in such a manner that tampering or removal of content during transport will be evident. In conflict-affected and high-risk areas, such physical security practices should be verifiable by appropriate and trusted third parties (*e.g.* customs authorities, independent auditors, Industry Programmes or Institutionalised Mechanisms).
3. Support the implementation of the principles and criteria set forth under the Extractive Industry Transparency Initiative (EITI).[18]

B. For local exporters, recyclers and international traders of Mined Gold and Recyclable Gold:

1. Assign unique internal reference numbers to all inputs and outputs, by bar, ingot and/or batch of gold accepted and produced, and affix and/or imprint that reference number on all outputs in such a manner that its tampering or removal will be evident.
2. Coordinate and support physical security practices used by other upstream companies. Promptly report any indications of tampering with shipments, and unseal and open shipments only by authorised personnel.
3. Preliminarily inspect all shipments for conformity to the information provided by the supplier on the *types of gold*, such as alluvial gold, gold doré, unprocessed recyclable gold or melted recyclable gold. Verify weight and quality information provided by the gold producer and/or shipper, and make a business record of such verification. Report any inconsistency between initial inspection of a shipment and information provided by the shipper promptly to internal security and those responsible in the company for due diligence, with no further action taken until the inconsistency is resolved.
4. Physically segregate and secure any shipment for which there is an unresolved inconsistency.

18. For information on the EITI, see *http://eiti.org/*. For a guide on how business can support EITI, see http://eiti.org/document/businessguide.

5. Seek to deal directly with legitimate artisanal and small-scale gold producers or their representatives where possible in order to exclude gold offered by persons that exploit them.

C. For refiners:

1. Assign unique internal reference numbers to all input and output, by bar, ingot and/or batch of gold accepted and produced, which should correspond to all the information collected on that gold input and output and generated through due diligence, including supplier "KYC" information and the origin of gold.
2. Coordinate and support physical security practices used by other upstream companies. Promptly report any indications of tampering with shipments, and unseal and open shipments only by authorised personnel.
3. Preliminarily inspect all shipments for conformity to the information provided by the supplier on the types of gold, such as alluvial gold, gold doré, unprocessed recyclable gold or melted recyclable gold. Verify weight and quality information provided by gold producer and/or shipper, and make a business record of such verification.
4. Report any inconsistency between initial inspection of a shipment and information provided by shipper promptly to refiner security and those responsible in the company for due diligence, with no further action taken until the inconsistency is resolved.
5. Physically segregate and secure any shipment for which there is an unresolved inconsistency.
6. Record, and render all gold outputs identifiable (*e.g.* by physically imprinting gold products, and/or affixing to packing material in such a manner that its tampering or removal will be evident) with the following information:
   a) Name and/or stamp/logo of the refiner.
   b) Year of refining/production.
   c) A unique reference allocated to each output (*e.g.* serial numbers, electronic identification or other practicable means).

D. For bullion banks:

1. Create inventory lists for all gold held by bullion banks, which include information on when each piece of gold was received and from whom.[19] These should include records of grandfathered stocks.

19. Full information usually included on inventory lists include: Batch Name; Receive Date; Metal; Type (*e.g.* large gold bars); Serial Number; Good Delivery / Non-Good Delivery; Total Number of Pallets; Total Number of Items; Current Weight; Pallet; Bar; Refiner; Gross Weight; Assay.

2. Provide, where possible, gold in accordance with customer requests for specific refiners whose due diligence practices have been independently verified to be consistent with this Guidance.
3. Maintain records of information imprinted on gold and the transaction numbers of when downstream companies take physical delivery of gold.
4. Upon request, provide the information imprinted on gold and physical delivery transaction numbers to direct downstream companies that take physical delivery of that gold.

E. For all other downstream companies (*e.g.* downstream users of gold and of gold materials and manufacturers of articles that contain gold):

1. Request suppliers provide the identification of the upstream gold refiner/s for gold-bearing materials and products, either by direct sourcing or via marks imprinted on a refined gold product if available, or from information provided by other downstream product suppliers or bullion banks.
2. If gold refiner/s are identified, request verification that the refiner/s has conducted due diligence in accordance with this Supplement. Where possible, seek reference to recognised audits by Industry Programmes or Institutionalised Mechanisms that incorporate in their auditing protocols the standards and processes contained in the Guidance.
3. Pass on information on the identification of the upstream gold refiner/s for gold-bearing materials and products to downstream customers.

STEP 2: IDENTIFY AND ASSESS RISKS IN THE SUPPLY CHAIN

OBJECTIVE: To identify and assess risks on the circumstances of extraction, consolidation, transport, trading, and export of gold from conflict-affected and high-risk areas.

Companies in the gold supply chain should use the strong management system put in place under Step 1 to identify and assess risks that the gold they produce or purchase through their supply chains may be contributing to conflict or serious human rights abuses.

All companies may cooperate to carry out the recommendations in this section through joint initiatives. However, companies retain individual responsibility for their due diligence, and should ensure that all joint work duly takes into consideration circumstances specific to the individual company.

SECTION I – RISK ASSESSMENT FOR MEDIUM AND LARGE-SCALE GOLD MINING COMPANIES AND ARTISANAL AND SMALL-SCALE MINING ENTERPRISES ("GOLD PRODUCERS")

A. **Determine whether the gold producer mines or transports any gold in a conflict-affected or high-risk area ("red flagged operations").** To do so, review the context of each location of gold origin and transport, relying on evidence from credible sources,[20] and use good faith efforts to make reasonable determinations based on the definition of conflict-affected and high-risk areas provided in the Introduction to this Supplement.

1. If the gold producer can reasonably determine on the basis of the information collected under Step 1 that it does not mine or transport any gold in a conflict-affected or high-risk area, no additional due diligence is required. The management systems established in Step 1 should be maintained and regularly reviewed.
2. If the gold producer determines that it produces or transports gold in a conflict-affected or high-risk area, *proceed to Step 2(B)*.

20. Review research reports from governments, international organisations, NGOs, and media, maps, UN reports and UN Security Council sanctions, industry literature relating to mineral extraction, and its impact on conflict, human rights or environmental harm in the country of potential origin, or other public statements (*e.g.* from ethical pension funds). Companies should also refer to any criteria and indicators of conflict-affected and high-risk areas developed through multi-stakeholder initiatives, including ongoing work related to the implementation of this Guidance facilitated by the OECD.

B. Also determine whether the gold producer purchases any gold (*e.g.* gold of artisanal and small-scale origin) potentially from a conflict-affected or high-risk area. To do so:

1. Identify all mines and/or mine smelt houses where the gold producer purchases Mined Gold from other sources, which may include ASM Gold.
2. Review the "KYC" information of those suppliers generated in Step 1, and gain additional information on the origin and transport of those other sources of Mined Gold, relying on first-hand evidence and credible sources.
3. Use good faith efforts to identify the presence of any of the following 'red flags' in a supply chain for those other sources of Mined Gold.

Red flag locations of gold origin and transit:

The gold originates from or has been transported through a conflict-affected or high-risk area.

The gold is claimed to originate from a country that has limited known reserves or stocks, likely resources or expected production levels of gold (i.e. the declared volumes of gold from that country are out of keeping with its known reserves or expected production levels).

The gold is claimed to originate from a country through which gold from conflict-affected and high-risk areas is known or reasonably suspected to transit.

The gold is claimed to originate from recyclable/scrap or mixed sources and has been refined in a country where gold from conflict-affected and high-risk areas is known or reasonably suspected to transit.

In each of these location-based red flag considerations, the risk is increased when anti-money laundering laws, anti-corruption laws, customs controls and other relevant governmental oversight laws are weakly enforced; informal banking systems operate, and cash is extensively used.

Supplier red flags:

Suppliers or other known upstream companies operate in one of the above-mentioned red flag locations of gold origin and transit, or have shareholder or other interests in suppliers of gold from one of the above-mentioned red flag locations of gold origin and transit.

Suppliers or other known upstream companies are known to have sourced gold from a red flag location of gold origin and transit in the last 12 months.

Red flag circumstances:

Anomalies or unusual circumstances are identified through the information collected in Step 1 which give rise to a reasonable suspicion that the gold may contribute to conflict or serious abuses associated with the extraction, transport or trade of gold.

a) **No red flags identified:** If the gold producer can reasonably determine that these red flags do not arise in that supply chain, no additional due diligence is required for that supply chain. The management systems established in Step 1 should be maintained and regularly reviewed.

b) **Red flags identified or information unknown:** Any gold producer that identifies a red flag in its gold supply chain, or is unable to reasonably exclude one or more of these red flags from a gold supply chain, should proceed to Step 2 (C) below.

C. Map the factual circumstances of the gold producer's red flagged operations and other sources of gold, under way and planned.

1. Undertake an in-depth review of the context of all red-flagged locations and the due diligence practices of any red flagged suppliers:

   a) Review research reports, including from governments, international organisations, NGOs, and media, maps, UN reports and UN Security Council sanctions, industry literature relating to gold extraction, and its impact on conflict, human rights or environmental harm in the country of potential origin, or other public statements (*e.g.* from ethical pension funds).

   b) Consult with a combination of local and central governments, local civil society organisations, community networks, UN peacekeeping units, and local suppliers. Respond to specific questions or requests for clarifications made by cooperating companies.

   c) Determine (including through desk research; in-site visits to gold suppliers; random sample verification of purchase records proportional to risk; and a review and assessment of purchase and anti-money laundering and counter terrorist financing (AML-CFT) procedures and directives, if applicable) if upstream suppliers have policies and management systems that are consistent with this Guidance and that such policies and management systems are operative.

2. **Establish on-the-ground assessment teams.** Gold producers with red flagged operations or other sources of Mined Gold should establish an on-the-ground assessment team (hereafter "assessment team") to generate and maintain information on the circumstances of gold extraction, trade,

handling, refining and export (see below). Gold producers remain individually responsible for ensuring that the requisite data is gathered, but may wish to facilitate this by establishing such a team jointly in cooperation with their customers or other companies in the upstream supply chain supplying from, or operating in these areas, or via an Industry Programme or Institutionalised Mechanism. Where 'joint' teams are not possible, or companies would prefer not to work jointly, companies should conduct on-the-ground assessments independently. Companies and other concerned stakeholders establishing on-the-ground assessment teams should:

a) Consider the following factors when contributing to joint on-the-ground assessments with other companies: the size of the contributing company and the resources available to conduct due diligence; each company's ability to access on-the-ground information and the position of the company in the supply chain; and the reliability of the company's due diligence, as demonstrated by cross-checking the data provided by the company on all gold inputs.[21]

b) Ensure that assessors are independent from the activity being assessed and free from conflict of interests.[22] Company assessors must commit to reporting truthfully and accurately and upholding the highest professional ethical standards and exercise "due professional care".[23]

c) Ensure the appropriate level of competence, by employing experts with knowledge and skill in as many of the following areas: the operational contexts assessed (*e.g.* linguistic abilities, cultural sensitivities), the substance of conflict-related risks (*e.g.* the standards in Annex II, human rights, international humanitarian law, corruption, financial crime, conflict and financing parties to a conflict, transparency), the nature and form of the gold supply chain, and the standards and process contained in this Guidance.

d) Provide assessment teams with access to mines, intermediaries, consolidators and/or transporters within the company's control or influence, including:

i) physical access to sites, including in other countries where trans-shipment or relabeling is likely;

21. For example, for gold from large-scale gold mines, the gold producer may be best situated to collect the relevant on-the-ground information at the mine site, while the other upstream companies ensure that the information is collected and maintained in accordance with this Guidance and should collect additional information on circumstances between gold producers and refiners.
22. Art 4, ISO 19011: 2002
23. Art 4, ISO 19011: 2002

ii) access to books, records or other evidence of procurement practices, tax, fee and royalty payments, and export documentation;

iii) local logistics support and assistance;

iv) security for itself and for any information providers.

e) Establish or support the creation, where appropriate, of community-monitoring networks and/or multi-stakeholder information units to feed information into the assessment team. Review, and add to or create if possible, interactive maps that indicate the location of mines, armed groups, trade routes, roadblocks and airfields.

3. **FOR LSM GOLD (WHETHER MINED BY MEDIUM AND LARGE SCALE MINING COMPANIES IN RED FLAGGED OPERATIONS OR LSM GOLD PURCHASED FROM OTHER SOURCES),** in order to determine risk, obtain evidence of the factual circumstances of gold extraction, processing, trade, handling, transport and export (if applicable), which may include:

a) Location and identity by name of all gold mines for every output.

b) Location of points where gold is processed, *e.g.*, consolidated, blended, crushed, milled and smelted into gold doré or alluvial gold output.

c) Methods of gold processing and transportation.

d) How gold is transported and processes in place to ensure integrity, with due regard taken of security concerns.

e) Location of transportation routes, points where gold is traded, and points of export and import where borders are crossed (if applicable).[24]

f) Current production and capacity of mine(s), a comparative analysis of mine capacity against recorded mine production, and record of any discrepancies.

g) Current processing production and processing capacity of mine smelthouse(s), and a comparative analysis of processing capacity against recorded processing production, and record of any discrepancies.

h) Identification and "know your counterparty" information of all third party service providers handling the gold (*e.g.* logistics, processors and

24. In cases where transporters do not wish to disclose this information for security concerns, upstream companies should ensure that transporters carry out a risk assessment on those transportation routes in line with this Guidance. Upstream companies should request a report from transporters detailing their findings from the risk assessment of transportation routes (i.e. the risks identified and steps taken to manage those risks). Upstream companies should report on those risks as outlined in Step 5. In cases where upstream companies are not using transporters, or are able to obtain information on the transportation routes, they should carry out the risk assessment of transportation routes themselves and report on those risks as outlined in Step 5.

transportation companies) or providing security at mine sites and along transportation routes. The identification should comprise the following measures, but the extent to which such measures are carried out should be determined on a risk sensitive basis:

i) identification of the ownership (including beneficial ownership) and corporate structure of the companies, including the names of corporate officers and directors;

ii) identification of the related businesses, subsidiaries, parents, affiliates;

iii) verification of the identity of the companies using reliable, independent source documents, data or information (*e.g.* business registers, extract, certificate of incorporation);

iv) checking government watchlist information (*e.g.* UN sanctions lists, OFAC Specially Designated Nationals Lists, World-Check search);

v) identification of any affiliation of the company with the government, political parties, the military, criminal networks or non-state armed groups, including any reported instances of affiliation with non-state armed groups and/or public or private security forces.

i) Operating licenses, *e.g.* mining, export.

j) All taxes, fees or royalties paid to government related to the extraction, trade, transport and export of gold.

k) All payments or compensation made to government agencies and officials related to the extraction, trade, transport and export of gold.

l) All payments made to public or private security forces or other armed groups at all points in the supply chain from extraction onwards, unless prohibited under applicable law.

m) The security services provided at the mine sites, transportation routes and all points where gold is handled or processed.

n) The training of security personnel and its conformity with the Voluntary Principles on Security and Human Rights.

o) Screening and security risks assessments of all security personnel in accordance with the Voluntary Principles on Security and Human Rights.

p) Militarisation of mine sites, transportation routes and points where gold is traded and exported.

q) Evidence of any serious abuses (torture, cruel, inhuman and degrading treatment, forced or compulsory labour, the worst forms of child labour, gross human rights violations, war crimes, or other serious violations of international humanitarian law, crimes against humanity or genocide) committed by any party in mines, transportation routes and points where gold is traded and/or processed.

r) Information on any direct or indirect support to non-state armed groups or public or private security forces (see Definitions).

s) If relevant, the number and name of sites where any artisanal and small-scale miners operate on the gold producer's concession, an estimate of the number of miners and an assessment of whether they can be considered to be involved in Legitimate Artisanal and Small-Scale Mining (see Definitions).

t) If relevant, instances of conflict or tensions in the relationship between medium and large-scale miners and artisanal and small-scale miners.

u) If relevant, any instances, reports or suspicions that ASM gold, or gold from other sources, is being unknowingly introduced into the gold producer's processing operations (*e.g.* the mine smelthouse), and/or fraudulently represented as being mined by the gold producer.

4. ***FOR ASM GOLD (WHETHER MINED BY ARTISANAL AND SMALL-SCALE MINING ENTERPRISES IN RED FLAGGED OPERATIONS OR PURCHASED BY MEDIUM AND LARGE-SCALE GOLD MINING COMPANIES),*** obtain evidence of the factual circumstances of gold extraction, processing, trade, handling, transport and export (if applicable). Companies should complement the steps they are taking to progressively collect the following information by referring to Step 3(C) and the Appendix of this Supplement to assist and enable artisanal and small-scale miners to build secure, transparent and verifiable gold supply chains:

a) Identification of the suppliers of all other sources of Mined Gold using reliable, independent source documents, data or information; any information on the government, political or military affiliations of those suppliers including in particular any reported instances of affiliation with non-state armed groups and/or public or private security forces; and the geographic sourcing area those suppliers.

b) The mine(s) of origin, transportation routes and points where gold is traded.

c) The artisanal mining team or association, and an assessment of whether they can be considered to be involved in Legitimate Artisanal and Small-Scale Mining (see Definitions).

d) Methods of gold processing and transportation.

e) Taxes, royalties and fees paid to government agencies and officials.

f) Identification and "know your counterparty" information of all third party service providers handling the gold (*e.g.* logistics, processors and transportation companies) or providing security at mine sites and along transportation routes. The identification should comprise the following measures, but the extent to which such measures are carried out should be determined on a risk sensitive basis:

i) identification of the ownership (including beneficial ownership) and corporate structure, including the names of corporate officers and directors);

ii) identification of the related businesses, subsidiaries, parents, affiliates;

iii) verification of the identity of the companies using reliable, independent source documents, data or information (*e.g.* business registers, extract, certificate of incorporation);

iv) checking government watchlist information (*e.g.* UN sanctions lists, OFAC Specially Designated Nationals Lists, World-Check search);

v) identification of any affiliation of the company with the government, political parties, military, criminal networks or non-state armed groups, including in particular any reported instances of affiliation with non-state armed groups and/or public or private security forces.

g) Militarisation of mine sites, transportation routes and points where gold is traded and exported.

h) Evidence of any serious abuses (torture, cruel, inhuman and degrading treatment, forced or compulsory labour, the worst forms of child labour, gross human rights violations, war crimes, or other serious violations of international humanitarian law, crimes against humanity or genocide) committed by any party in mines, transportation routes and points where gold is traded and/or processed.[25]

i) Information on any direct or indirect support to non-state armed groups or public or private security forces through the extraction, transport, trade, handling or export of gold.

j) Instances of conflict or tensions in the relationship between medium and large-scale miners and artisanal and small-scale miners.

k) Any instances, reports or suspicions that gold from other sources is being unknowingly introduced into the gold supply chain, and/or fraudulently represented.

D. Assess risks in the supply chain. Assess the information collected and learned through mapping the factual circumstances of the company's red

25. See paragraph 1, Annex II of the OECD Due Diligence Guidance (2011).

flagged supply chain(s). The company should consider a "risk" any reasonable inconsistency between the information obtained and the following:

1. The company supply chain policy, consistent with Annex II of this Guidance.[26]
2. The due diligence standards and processes contained in this Guidance, as well as information obtained through Step 1 of this Guidance.
3. National laws of the countries where the company is domiciled or publicly-traded (if applicable). of the countries from which the gold is likely to originate; and of transit or re-export countries.
4. Legal instruments governing company operations and business relations, such as financing agreements, contractor agreements, and supplier agreements.
5. Other relevant international instruments, such as the OECD Guidelines for Multinational Enterprises, international human rights and humanitarian law and international anti-money laundering recommendations and guidance.

SECTION II – RISK ASSESSMENT FOR LOCAL EXPORTERS, RECYCLERS, INTERNATIONAL TRADERS OF MINED/RECYCLABLE GOLD AND REFINERS

A. Determine Gold Origin. The assessment of risk in a supply chain begins with the origin of gold supply. Different origins have different risks and require different types of risk assessments (see *Figure 1 – Risks in the supply chain of gold from conflict-affected and high-risk areas* in the Introduction of the Supplement). All determinations of Gold Origin should be based on reasonable and good faith efforts of the company relying on evidence generated in Step 1 as well as additional first-hand evidence (collected through engagement with suppliers and desk research) and credible sources.[27] Local gold exporters, international gold traders and refiners should assess and verify representations of suppliers with steps

26. See Step 1 (A) above and Annex II.
27. Review research reports from governments, international organisations, NGOs, and media, maps, UN reports and UN Security Council sanctions, industry literature relating to mineral extraction, and its impact on conflict, human rights or environmental harm in the country of potential origin, or other public statements (*e.g.* from ethical pension funds). Companies should also refer to any criteria and indicators of conflict-affected and high-risk areas developed through multi-stakeholder initiatives.

proportional to risk in order to make reasonable determinations of Gold Origin.

1. **For Mined Gold,** *the origin is the mine itself,* whether artisanal and small-scale mine or a medium or large-scale mine.
   a) An exception to this is Mining Byproduct, such as gold obtained from the mining of copper, a mineral outside of the scope of this Guidance.[28] The origin of Mining Byproduct gold should be deemed to be the point where trace gold is first separated from its original mineral ore (*e.g.* the refinery). The refiner's due diligence should ensure that false representations are not made to hide the origin of newly mined gold through Mining Byproducts.
2. **For Recyclable Gold,** *the origin is the point at which it becomes recyclable* (i.e. *when the gold is collected for return into the gold industry to reclaim its metal value),* such as when it is first sold back to a gold recycler/refiner. The point at which the gold becomes recyclable new origin as recyclable gold should be reviewed by a refiner's due diligence, to exclude false representations made to hide the origin of newly mined gold.
3. ***Grandfathered Stocks,*** *if demonstrated by a "verifiable date" to have been created in their current form prior to 1 January 2012, do not require a determination of origin.* Only the presence of the "supplier red flags" (see below) should trigger additional due diligence on suppliers to ensure that the trade and sale of Grandfathered Stocks does not contravene United Nations sanctions resolutions or enable money-laundering resulting from, or connected to, the sale of gold reserves in conflict-affected and high-risk areas.

B. Identify Red Flags in the gold supply chain. Based on the information on Gold Origin, and information generated through Step 1 (including all "KYC" information on suppliers), companies should identify the presence of any of the following 'red flags' in a supply chain for mined, recyclable or existing stocks of gold:

Red flag locations of gold origin and transit:

The gold originates from or has been transported through a conflict-affected or high-risk area.

28. For example, trace gold in copper sulphide ore does not lead to production of gold in a form that is separate and independent of that ore until after the copper has been fully refined to 99.99% pure cathode copper. At that point the trace gold has become concentrated in residue electrolytic cell slimes to perhaps 2%, and those cell slimes are traded to gold refiners for their gold content.

The gold is claimed to originate from a country that has limited known reserves or stocks, likely resources or expected production levels of gold (i.e. the declared volumes of gold from that country are out of keeping with its known reserves or expected production levels).

The gold is claimed to originate from a country through which gold from conflict-affected and high-risk areas is known or reasonably suspected to transit.

The gold is claimed to originate from recyclable/scrap or mixed sources and has been refined in a country where gold from conflict-affected and high-risk areas is known or reasonably suspected to transit.

In each of these location-based red flag considerations, the risk is increased when anti-money laundering laws, anti-corruption laws, customs controls and other relevant governmental oversight laws are weakly enforced; informal banking systems operate, and cash is extensively used.

Supplier red flags:

Suppliers or other known upstream companies operate in one of the above-mentioned red flag locations of gold origin and transit, or have shareholder or other interests in suppliers of gold from one of the above-mentioned red flag locations of gold origin and transit.

Suppliers or other known upstream companies are known to have sourced gold from a red flag location of gold origin and transit in the last 12 months.

Red flag circumstances:

Anomalies or unusual circumstances are identified through the information collected in Step 1 which give rise to a reasonable suspicion that the gold may contribute to conflict or serious abuses associated with the extraction, transport or trade of gold.

a) **No red flags identified:** If the local gold exporter, international gold trader or refiner can reasonably determine that these red flags do not arise in that supply chain, no additional due diligence is required for that supply chain. The management systems established in Step 1 should be maintained and regularly reviewed.

b) **Red flags identified or information unknown:** Any local gold exporter, international gold trader or refiner that identifies a red flag in its gold supply chain, or is unable to reasonably exclude one or more of these red flags from a gold supply chain, should proceed to Step 2 (C) below.

C. Map the factual circumstances of the company's red flagged supply chain(s), under way and planned.

1. Undertake and in-depth review of the context of all red-flagged locations and the due diligence practices of any red flagged suppliers.
   a) Review research reports including from governments, international organisations, NGOs, and media, maps, UN reports and UN Security Council sanctions, industry literature relating to mineral extraction, and its impact on conflict, human rights or environmental harm in the country of potential origin, or other public statements (*e.g.* from ethical pension funds).
   b) Consult with a combination of local and central governments, local civil society organisations, community networks, UN peacekeeping units, and local suppliers. Respond to specific questions or requests for clarifications made by cooperating companies.
   c) Determine (including through desk research; in-site visits to gold suppliers; random sample verification of purchase records proportional to risk; and a review and assessment of purchase and anti-money laundering and counter terrorist financing (AML-CFT) procedures and directives, if applicable) if upstream suppliers have policies and management systems that are consistent with this Guidance and that such policies and management systems are operative.
2. ***FOR MINED GOLD,* establish on-the-ground assessment teams.** Local gold exporters, international gold traders or refiners with identified red flags remain in all circumstances individually responsible for ensuring that the information on the factual circumstances of the company's red flagged supply chain(s) is gathered. Local gold exporters, international gold traders or refiners with identified red flags in their supply chains should establish on-the-ground assessment teams to generate and maintain information on suppliers (if relevant) the circumstances of mineral extraction, trade, handling, refining and export. Upstream companies may establish such a team jointly in cooperation with other upstream companies supplying from, or operating in these areas, or via an industry or multi-stakeholder mechanism or initiative. Where 'joint' teams are not possible, or companies would prefer not to work jointly, companies should conduct on-the-ground assessments independently. Companies and other stakeholders establishing on-the-ground assessment teams should:
   a) Consider the following factors when contributing to joint on-the-ground assessments: the size of the cooperating companies and the resources available to conduct due diligence; the ability to access on the ground information and the position of the company in the supply chain; the quality of any previously established on-the-ground assessment teams

of other upstream companies, including gold producers; and the reliability of the company's due diligence, as demonstrated by cross-checking the data provided by the company on all gold inputs.[29]

b) Ensure that assessors are independent from the activity being assessed and free from conflict of interests.[30] Company assessors must commit to reporting truthfully and accurately and upholding the highest professional ethical standards and exercise "due professional care".[31]

c) Ensure the appropriate level of competence, by employing experts with knowledge and skill in as many of the following areas: the operational contexts assessed (*e.g.* linguistic abilities, cultural sensitivities), the substance of conflict-related risks (*e.g.* the standards in Annex II, human rights, international humanitarian law, corruption, financial crime, conflict and financing parties to a conflict, transparency), the nature and form of the gold supply chain, and the standards and process contained in this due diligence Guidance.

d) Provide assessment teams with access to mines, intermediaries, consolidators and/or transporters within the company's control or influence, including:

i) physical access to sites, including in other countries where trans-shipment or relabeling is likely;

ii) access to books, records or other evidence of procurement practices, tax, fee and royalty payments, and export documentation;

iii) local logistics support and assistance;

iv) security for itself and for any information providers.

e) Establish or support the creation, where appropriate, of community-monitoring networks and/or multi-stakeholder information units to feed information into the assessment team. Review, and add to or create if possible, interactive maps that indicate the location of mines, armed groups, trade routes, roadblocks and airfields.

3. ***FOR MINED GOLD,*** determine if the Mined Gold is LSM Gold or ASM Gold.

a) ***For LSM Gold,*** cooperate with medium and large-scale gold producers to obtain evidence, where applicable to the position of the company in the

29. For example, for gold from large-scale gold mines, the gold producer may be best situated to collect the relevant on-the-ground information at the mine site, while the other upstream companies ensure that the information is collected and maintained in accordance with this Guidance and should collect any available additional information on circumstances between gold producers and refiners.
30. Art 4, ISO 19011: 2002
31. Art 4, ISO 19011: 2002

supply chain, of the factual circumstances of gold extraction, trade, handling and export, which may include:

i) Location and identity by name of all gold mines for every output.

ii) Location of points where gold is processed, *e.g.*, consolidated, blended, crushed, milled and smelted into gold doré or alluvial gold output.

iii) Methods of gold processing and transportation.

iv) Location of transportation routes, points where gold is traded, and points of export and import where borders are crossed (if applicable).[32]

v) Current production and capacity of mine(s), a comparative analysis of mine capacity against recorded mine production if possible, and record any discrepancies.

vi) Current processing production and processing capacity of mine smelthouse(s), and a comparative analysis of processing capacity against recorded processing production if possible, and record of any discrepancies.

vii) Identification and "know your counterparty" information of all actors in the upstream supply chain, including, but not limited to, the gold producers, intermediaries, gold traders and exporters and re-exporters, as well as third party service providers handling the gold (*e.g.* logistics, processors and transportation companies) or providing security at mine sites and along transportation routes. The identification should comprise the following measures, but the extent to which such measures are carried out should be determined on a risk sensitive basis:

1. identification of the ownership (including beneficial ownership) of the companies and corporate structure, including the names of corporate officers and directors);
2. identification of the related businesses, subsidiaries, parents, affiliates;

32. In cases where transporters do not wish to disclose this information for security concerns, upstream companies should ensure that transporters carry out a risk assessment on those transportation routes in line with this Guidance. Upstream companies should request a report from transporters detailing their findings from the risk assessment of transportation routes (i.e. the risks identified and steps taken to manage those risks). Upstream companies should report on those risks as outlined in Step 5. In cases where upstream companies are not using transporters, or are able to obtain information on the transportation routes, they should carry out the risk assessment of transportation routes themselves and report on those risks as outlined in Step 5.

3. verification of the identity of the companies using reliable, independent source documents, data or information (*e.g.* business registers extract, certificate of incorporation);
4. checking government watchlist information (*e.g.* UN sanctions lists, OFAC Specially Designated Nationals Lists, World-Check search);
5. identification of any affiliation of the company with the government, political parties, military, criminal networks or non-state armed groups, , including any reported instances of affiliation with non-state armed groups and/or public or private security forces.

viii) Operating licenses, *e.g.* mining, export.

ix) All taxes, fees or royalties paid to government related to the extraction, trade, transport and export of gold.

x) All payments or compensation made to government agencies and officials related to the extraction, trade, transport and export of gold.

xi) All payments made to public or private security forces or other armed groups at all points in the supply chain from extraction onwards, unless prohibited under applicable law.

xii) The security services provided at the mine sites, transportation routes and all points where gold is handled or processed.

xiii) The training of security personnel, and the conformity of that training with the Voluntary Principles on Security and Human Rights.

xiv) Screening and security risks assessments of all security personnel in accordance with the Voluntary Principles on Security and Human Rights.

xv) Militarisation of mine sites, transportation routes and points where gold is traded and exported.

xvi) Evidence of any serious abuses (torture, cruel, inhuman and degrading treatment, forced or compulsory labour, the worst forms of child labour, gross human rights violations, war crimes, or other serious violations of international humanitarian law, crimes against humanity or genocide) committed by any party in mines, transportation routes and points where gold is traded and/or processed.

xvii) Information on any direct or indirect support to non-state armed groups or public or private security forces (see Definitions).

xviii) If relevant, the number and name of sites where artisanal and small-scale miners operate on the gold producers concession, and an estimate of the number of miners and an assessment of whether they can be considered to be involved in Legitimate Artisanal and Small-Scale Mining (see Definitions).

xix) If relevant, instances of conflict or tensions in the relationship between medium and large-scale miners and artisanal and small-scale miners.

xx) If relevant, any instances, reports or suspicions that ASM gold, or gold from other sources, is being unknowingly introduced into gold producer's processing operations (*e.g.* the mine smelthouse), and/or fraudulently represented as being mined by the gold producer.

b) ***For ASM Gold,*** obtain evidence of the factual circumstances of gold extraction, trade, handling and export. Companies should complement the steps they are taking to progressively collect the following information by referring to Step 3(C) and the Appendix to assist and enable artisanal and small-scale miners to build secure, transparent and verifiable gold supply chains:

i) Identification of the suppliers of ASM Gold to the local gold exporter using reliable, independent source documents, data or information; any information on the government, political or military affiliations of those suppliers including in particular any reported instances of affiliation with non-state armed groups and/or public or private security forces; and the geographic sourcing area those suppliers.

ii) The mine(s) of origin, the transportation routes and points where gold is traded.

iii) The artisanal mining team or association, and an assessment of whether they can be considered to be involved in Legitimate Artisanal and Small-Scale Mining (see Definitions).

iv) The methods of gold processing and transportation.

v) Taxes, royalties and fees paid to government institutions and officials on export.

vi) Identification and "know your counterparty" information (where applicable) of the gold exporter and all actors in the supply chain from the gold exporter to the refiner, including international gold traders and all third party service providers handling the gold (*e.g.* logistics, processors and transportation companies) or providing security at mine sites and along transportation routes. The identification should comprise the following measures, but the extent to which such measures are carried out should be determined on a risk sensitive basis:

1. identification of the ownership (including beneficial ownership) and corporate structure, including the names of corporate officers and directors);
2. identification of the related businesses, subsidiaries, parents, affiliates;
3. verification of the identity of the companies using reliable, independent source documents, data or information (*e.g.* business registers, extract, certificate of incorporation);
4. checking government watchlist information (*e.g.* UN sanctions lists, OFAC Specially Designated Nationals Lists, World-Check search);
5. identification of any affiliation of the company with the government, political parties, military, criminal networks or non-state armed groups, including in particular any reported instances of affiliation with non-state armed groups and/or public or private security forces.

vii) Militarisation of mine sites, transportation routes and points where gold is traded and exported.

viii) Evidence of any serious abuses (torture, cruel, inhuman and degrading treatment, forced or compulsory labour, the worst forms of child labour, gross human rights violations, war crimes, or other serious violations of international humanitarian law, crimes against humanity or genocide) committed by any party in mines, transportation routes and points where gold is traded and/or processed.[33]

ix) Information on any direct or indirect support to non-state armed groups or public or private security forces through the extraction, transport, trade, handling or export of gold (see Definitions).

x) Any instances, reports or suspicions that gold from other sources is being unknowingly introduced into the gold supply chain, and/or fraudulently represented.

xi) If relevant, instances of conflict or tensions in the relationship between medium and large-scale miners and artisanal and small-scale miners.

4. **FOR RECYCLABLE GOLD,**[34] collect additional information (including through desk research, in-site visits to gold suppliers and random sample

33. See paragraph 1, Annex II of the OECD Due Diligence Guidance (2011).
34. Recycled material is not itself a concern for contributing to conflict, however, recycled material is a potential means of laundering gold that has been mined in conflict-affected and high-risk areas in order to hide its origin.

verification of purchase records proportional to risk) for Recyclable Gold from red flagged supply chains of Recyclable Gold using a risk-based approach,[35] with priority given to persons, places and transactions that present higher risk. As an important part of risk-based due diligence, suppliers and transactions should be identified and records made and maintained at all levels. Such risk factors include, but are not limited to:

a) **Value of a transaction.** Beginning with the threshold of 15,000 US dollars[36] for any transaction of recyclable gold outside a conflict-affected or high-risk area, due diligence should be proportional to increasing value. However, transactions at or near a mining area may include very small amounts, *e.g.*, one gram of gold. Therefore any transactions of recyclable gold inside a conflict-affected or high-risk area, regardless of value, should attract enhanced scrutiny.

b) **Place of a transaction.** Gold is valuable in small quantities and easily transported, so no place is completely risk-free but higher risk places of transactions include places where the location(s) of gold transit and export are not reasonably reconciled with the declared location of gold origin; where there is ready access to competitive markets or processing operations closer to the declared location of gold origin; where AML/CFT laws, anti-corruption laws, customs controls and other relevant governmental oversight laws are weakly enforced; and where informal banking systems operate in the country, including cash-based economies.[37]

c) **Type of material.** Unprocessed Recyclable Gold is not as likely a vehicle for laundering mined gold from conflict-affected and high-risk areas as Melted Recyclable Gold (see Definitions), although there are cases where the Unprocessed Recyclable Gold originates from areas where there is a known practice of fabricating gold products directly from Mined Gold as a means of tax avoidance or laundering gold. Mined Gold that has been produced in a conflict area at a high concentration (*e.g.*, 90% pure from alluvial mining) is unlikely to be laundered through lower value materials that require many more processes to upgrade and refine, as

35. While these records would not necessarily accompany materials in movement through the supply chain, they should be available for subsequent tracking and verification. Governments and companies in gold supply chains should refer to the Financial Action Task Force 40 Recommendations to combat money laundering and terrorist finance, and specifically to its RBA Guidance for Dealers in Precious Metal and Stones (June 2008).
36. See Financial Action Task Force (FATF), 40 Recommendations (2003) and Financial Action Task Force, *RBA Guidance for Dealers in Precious Metal and Stones*, 17 June 2008.
37. Refer, Financial Action Task Force, *RBA Guidance for Dealers in Precious Metal and Stones*, 17 June 2008, para. 109.

well as significantly longer time for production of marketable gold. Examples of low value materials that are not likely to be laundering vehicles would be electronic scrap or residue cell slimes from refining of other metals. High concentration gold jewellery, on the other hand, may have similar physical characteristics to mined conflict gold.

d) **Unusual circumstances.** Material claimed to be recycled should be considered for its reasonableness in context. For example, sudden unusual increases in volume of high-grade material from a supplier or area should be explained. If jewellery worn in a country is typically 14k (58%), an offer claimed to be recycled jewellery at 90% should be questioned.

e) **Supplier.** Different suppliers of recyclable gold will present varying levels of risk for laundering-type activities. For example recyclable gold produced on a controlled facility during manufacturing/processing presents lower risks than a collector sourcing recyclable gold from multiple sources. Other high-risk factors include any reasonable inconsistency between the recommended due diligence processes of this Guidance and the practices of suppliers; or the supplier "has significant and unexplained geographic distance" from a supplier or counterparty in the supply chain.

5. ***FOR RECYCLABLE GOLD,*** collect the following information of those transactions requiring enhanced scrutiny, including through desk research, in-site visits to gold suppliers, random sample verification of purchase records proportional to risk, and a more in-depth review and assessment of purchase and anti-money laundering and counter terrorist financing (AML-CFT) procedures and directives, if applicable:

a) Whether there are manufacturing facilities where scrap may be generated.

b) Whether there is significant ownership and turnover of privately-held gold jewellery.

c) Determine, through in-site visits and examination of documents, the reasonably approximate level of business being done in recyclable/scrap gold, recognising that it will vary, particularly with the price of gold and economic conditions.

D. Assess risks in the supply chain. Assess the information collected and learned through mapping the factual circumstances of the company's red flagged supply chain(s). The company should consider a "risk" any reasonable inconsistency between the information obtained and the following:

1. The standards of the company supply chain policy, consistent with Annex II;[38]
2. The due diligence standards and processes contained in this Guidance;
3. National laws of the countries where the company is domiciled or publicly-traded (if applicable); of the countries from which the gold is likely to originate; and of transit or re-export countries;
4. Legal instruments governing company operations and business relations, such as financing agreements, contractor agreements, and supplier agreements;
5. Other relevant international instruments, such as the OECD Guidelines for Multinational Enterprises, international human rights and humanitarian law and international anti-money laundering recommendations and guidance.

SECTION III – RISK ASSESSMENT FOR DOWNSTREAM COMPANIES

Downstream companies should identify the risks in their supply chain by assessing the due diligence practices of their refiners against this Guidance.

A. Identify, to the best of their efforts, the refiner(s) of gold in their supply chain(s). Downstream companies should aim to identify the gold refiners that produce the refined gold used in their supply chain. Gold refiners can be identified upon requests through the downstream chain of suppliers, however downstream companies should assess and verify representations of suppliers with steps proportional to risk. In some cases, the gold will already have the refiner's mark imprinted on the bar, coin, rod or other refined gold product.

1. ***Refiners identified*** *– Proceed to Step 2, Section III (B).*
2. ***Unable to identify refiners after best efforts*** *– Proceed to Step 3, Section II.*

B. Obtain preliminary evidence of the refiner's due diligence to see whether they have identified, or reasonably should have identified red flags in their supply chains. All determination of whether refiners have, or reasonably should have, identified red flags in their supply chains should be based on reasonable and good faith efforts of the company relying on evidence generated in Step 1 as well as any additional information (collected through engagement with suppliers and

38. See Step 1 (A) above and Annex II.

desk research). Companies should verify representations of suppliers with external sources of evidence proportional to risk in order to make reasonable determinations.

1. ***Refiner has not identified any red flags:*** If a downstream company in a gold supply chain can reasonably determine that these red flags do not arise in that refiner's supply chain, no additional due diligence is required for that supply chain. The management systems established in Step 1 should be maintained and regularly reviewed.
2. ***Refiner has identified red flags in their gold supply chain, or does not know:*** Any downstream company that identifies a red flag in their refiner's gold supply chain, or is unable to reasonably exclude one or more of these red flags from their refiner's gold supply chain, should proceed to Step 2, Part III (C).

C. Assess risks by evaluating the supply chain due diligence practices of refiners with red flags in their gold supply chains. In order to carry out risk assessments, companies should assess whether the refiners with red flags in their supply chain have carried out all elements of due diligence for responsible supply chains of gold from conflict-affected and high-risk areas recommended in this Guidance. Downstream companies should:

1. Gain evidence on gold supply chain due diligence practices of the refiners.
2. Review the information generated by any risk assessment teams.
3. Cross-check evidence of due diligence practices of the refiners against the supply chain policy and due diligence processes contained in this Guidance. The company should consider any reasonable inconsistency between the due diligence practices of suppliers and the company supply chain policy (consistent with Annex II) as a risk that should be acted on in Step 3.
4. Determine whether the refiner's due diligence practices have been audited against a standard in conformance with this Guidance, and obtain the results of that audit. *In cases where the refiner's diligence practices have not been audited against a standard in conformance with this Guidance*, or where any inconsistency between the refiner's due diligence and the standards and processes in this Guidance is found, downstream companies should seek to manage risks in accordance with Step 3, and seek to source from refiners that are audited in accordance with Step 4 of this Guidance.

STEP 3: DESIGN AND IMPLEMENT A STRATEGY TO RESPOND TO IDENTIFIED RISKS

OBJECTIVE: To evaluate and respond to identified risks in order to prevent or mitigate adverse impacts. Companies may cooperate to carry out the recommendations in this section through joint initiatives. However, companies retain individual responsibility for their due diligence, and should ensure that all joint work duly takes into consideration circumstances specific to the individual company.

SECTION I – RISK MANAGEMENT FOR UPSTREAM COMPANIES

A. Report findings to designated senior management, outlining the information gathered and the actual and potential risks identified in the supply chain risk assessment.

B. Enhance engagement with suppliers and the internal systems of transparency, information collection and control over the gold supply chain from Step 1(C). Upstream companies should:

1. Establish a chain of custody and/or traceability system that collects and maintains disaggregated information outlined in Step 2, Section I and II, (C) for all gold input and output from a red flagged supply chain.
2. Enhance physical security practices as appropriate to the circumstances (*e.g.* security of transport, sealing in tamper-proof containers, etc.) over any discrepancies noted in mine production and capacity, processing production and capacity, or information provided by suppliers on gold shipments.
3. Physically segregate and secure any shipment for which there is an identified risk of association with conflict and serious abuses of human rights.
4. Incorporate the right to conduct unannounced spot-checks on suppliers and have access to their relevant documentation into commercial contracts and/or written agreements with suppliers which can be applied and monitored.[39]

39. See steps 2-5 for information on monitoring suppliers and managing non-compliance.

5. For every gold input, share the following information gained and maintained by the assessment team throughout the upstream supply chain:
   a) the mine of origin, with the greatest possible specificity;
   b) locations where gold or gold-bearing material is consolidated, blended, crushed, milled, smelted and refined;
   c) the method of extraction (artisanal and small-scale or medium and large-scale mining), and dates of concentrating, smelting and refining;
   d) the weight and assayed quality characteristics;
   e) the identity of all suppliers and relevant service providers handling the gold in the upstream supply chain from the mine of origin until the refiner; the ownership (including beneficial ownership); the corporate structure including the names of corporate officers and directors; the business, government, political or military affiliations of those companies and officers within conflict-affected and high-risk areas.
   f) all taxes, fees or royalties paid to government related to the extraction, trade, transport and export of gold;
   g) all payments or compensation made to government agencies and officials related to the extraction, trade, transport and export of gold;
   h) all payments made to public or private security forces or other armed groups at all points in the supply chain from extraction onwards, unless prohibited under applicable law;
   i) how gold is transported and processes in place to ensure integrity, with due regard taken of security concerns.
6. ***For refiners,*** make information generated through due diligence processes available to auditors for purposes of compliance with Industry Programmes[40] or Institutionalised Mechanisms, regional or global, once in place with the mandate to collect and process information on gold from conflict-affected and high-risk areas. Where no such programme or mechanism exists, make relevant information available to downstream purchasers.

C. Devise and adopt a risk management plan. Companies should adopt a supply chain risk management plan that outlines the company responses to risks identified in Step 2 in conformity to Annex II of the Guidance. Companies may manage risk by either *i)* continuing trade throughout the course of measurable risk mitigation efforts; *ii)* temporarily

40. See, for example, the LBMA Responsible Gold Guidance, the Conflict-Free Smelter Program and the RJC Chain-of-Custody Certification, if consistent with this Guidance.

suspending trade while pursuing ongoing measurable risk mitigation; or *iii)* disengaging with a supplier in cases where mitigation appears not feasible or unacceptable. To determine and devise a risk management strategy, companies should:

1. Review the model supply chain policy on gold from conflict-affected and high-risk areas in Annex II of the Guidance to determine whether the identified risks should be mitigated by continuing, suspending or terminating the relationship with suppliers.
2. Manage risks that do not require termination of the relationship with a supplier through measurable risk mitigation. Measurable risk mitigation should *aim to promote significant and measurable improvement within six months from the adoption of the risk management plan.* In devising a strategy for risk mitigation, companies should:
   a) Build and/or exercise leverage over the actors in the supply chain who can most effectively and most directly mitigate the risks of contributing to conflict. Upstream companies already may have actual or potential leverage over other upstream actors in the supply chain. Upstream companies should find ways to constructively engage with suppliers and relevant stakeholders and demonstrate significant and measurable improvement towards eliminating the risk within six months from the adoption of the risk management plan.[41]

   b) Consult with suppliers and affected stakeholders and agree on the strategy for measurable risk mitigation in the risk management plan. Measurable risk mitigation should be adjusted to the company's specific suppliers and the contexts of their operations, state clear performance objectives within six months from the adoption of the risk management plan and include qualitative and/or quantitative indicators to measure improvement.[42] Companies should ensure sufficient time for affected stakeholders to review the risk assessment and management plan and respond to and take due account of questions, concerns and alternative suggestions for risk management.

   c) Engage in or support, where appropriate, Industry Programmes or Institutionalised Mechanisms on responsible supply chain management while ensuring that these initiatives take due account of their social and

41. Companies should refer to Annex III of the Guidance for the recommended risk management strategy. Annex III includes suggested measures for risk mitigation and some recommended indicators to measure improvement. More detailed guidance on risk mitigation is expected to come from the implementation phase of the Guidance.
42. See Annex III of the Guidance, *Suggested Measures for Risk Mitigation and Indicators for Measuring Improvement.*

economic effects on developing countries and of existing internationally recognised standards.[43]

i) **All gold producers with red flagged operations as well as other upstream companies sourcing ASM Gold** should assist and enable Legitimate Artisanal and Small-Scale Mining producers (see Definitions) from whom they source to build secure, transparent and verifiable gold supply chains, consistent with the Appendix.

ii) All other gold producers with red flagged operations as well as other upstream companies are encouraged to support the suggested measures contained in the Appendix.

D. Implement the risk management plan, monitor and track performance of risk mitigation, report back to designated senior management and consider suspending or discontinuing engagement with a supplier after failed attempts at mitigation, in conformity with the recommended risk management strategies outlined in Annex II.[44] Upstream companies should implement, monitor and track performance of risk mitigation in cooperation and/or consultation with local and central authorities, upstream companies, international or civil society organisations and affected third parties as appropriate. Upstream companies may wish to establish or support the creation of community-monitoring networks to monitor or track performance of risk mitigation.

E. Undertake additional fact and risk assessments for risks requiring mitigation, or after a change of circumstances.[45] Supply chain due diligence is a dynamic process and requires on-going risk monitoring. After implementing a risk mitigation strategy, companies should repeat Step 2 to ensure effective management of risk. Additionally, any change in the company's supply chain may require some steps to be repeated in order to prevent or mitigate adverse impacts.

43. OECD Guidelines for Multinational Enterprises (2011), Chapter II (B)(2).
44. Companies should suspend or discontinue engagement with the supplier for a minimum of three months if within six months from the adoption of the risk management plan there is no significant measurable improvement to prevent or mitigate the identified risk.
45. A change of circumstances should be determined on a risk-sensitive basis through on-going monitoring of the companies' chain of custody documentation and the contexts of the conflict-affected areas of mineral origin and transport. Such change of circumstances may include a change of supplier or actor in the chain of custody, place of origin, transportation routes or point of export. It may also include factors specific to the context, such as an increase in conflict in specific areas, changes in military personnel overseeing an area and ownership or control changes in the mine of origin.

SECTION II – RISK MANAGEMENT FOR DOWNSTREAM COMPANIES

A. **Report findings to designated senior management,** outlining the information gathered and the actual and potential risks identified in the supply chain risk assessment.

B. **Enhance internal system of transparency, information collection and control over the gold supply chain from Step 1(C).** Include disaggregate and regularly updated information tracking the identity of refiners (where identified) and resulting due diligence findings from Step 2, Section III.

C. **Devise and adopt a risk management plan.** Companies should adopt a risk management plan that outlines the company responses to risks identified in Step 2. This strategy will differ depending on whether refiners in the supply chain have been identified or not:

1. ***Unable to identify refiners*** – If after reasonable steps and good faith efforts in Step 1 and 2, downstream companies are still unable to identify refiners in their supply chain(s), they should devise and adopt a risk management plan that will enable them to do so. Downstream companies should be able to demonstrate significant measurable improvement in their efforts towards identifying the refiners in their supply chain. Downstream companies may identify refiners in their supply chain(s) through individual efforts or collaborative industry schemes:
   - *a)* Downstream companies should identify refiners through confidential discussions with the companies' immediate suppliers, through the incorporation of confidential supplier disclosure requirements into supplier contracts and/or by using confidential-information-sharing systems.
   - *b)* Downstream companies that may find it difficult (due to their size or other factors) to identify actors upstream from their direct suppliers, may engage and actively cooperate with other industry members with which they share suppliers (or downstream companies with which they have a business relationship) to identify the refiners in their supply chain and assess their due diligence practices. They may also identify refiners through industry validation schemes that meet the requirements of this Guidance in order to source therefrom.
2. ***Refiners identified with red flag risks in their supply chain*** – Downstream companies may manage risk by either *i)* continuing trade with the refiner throughout the course of measurable risk mitigation carried out by the refiner in accordance with Annex II of the Guidance; *ii)* temporarily

suspending trade with the refiner while the refiner is pursuing ongoing measurable risk mitigation; or *iii)* disengaging with a refiner in cases where mitigation appears not feasible or where the refiner has failed to respond to risks in accordance with the risk management strategy outlined in Annex II:

a) Take immediate steps to disengage with a refiner (directly or through sub-suppliers) if the refiner has not immediately suspended or discontinued engagement with its suppliers where reasonable risks of serious abuses (see paragraphs 1 and 2 of Annex II) or direct or indirect support to non-state armed groups exist (see paragraphs 3 and 4 of Annex II).

b) When refiners are engaging in risk mitigation pursuant to Annex II[46] or where refiners are still in the process of fully implementing the due diligence recommendations contained in this Guidance, downstream companies should ensure refiners demonstrate significant and measurable improvement within six months from the adoption of their risk management plans. In devising their own risk management plans, downstream companies should:

i) Build and/or exercise leverage over the refiners with red flags in their supply chain(s), who may be able to more effectively and directly mitigate the risks of contributing to conflict. Downstream companies may build leverage over refiners through the inclusion of due diligence performance into contracts (where applicable), or working through industry associations and multi-stakeholder initiatives, while ensuring that these initiatives take due account of their social and economic effects on developing countries and of existing internationally recognised standards.[47]

ii) Focus efforts on improving the refiner's due diligence performance, through value orientation or capability-training. Downstream companies should also encourage their own and upstream industry membership organisations to develop and implement due diligence capability-training modules in cooperation with relevant international organisations, NGOs, stakeholders and other experts.

iii) Consult with refiners and other common suppliers to agree on measurable risk mitigation in the risk management plan. Measurable risk mitigation should be adjusted to the company's specific suppliers and the contexts of their operations, state clear performance objectives

46. See Paragraphs 10 and 14 of Annex II of the Guidance on risk management of direct or indirect support to public or private security forces, bribery and fraudulent misrepresentation of the origin of minerals, money-laundering and payment of taxes, fees and royalties to governments.
47. Chapter II (B)(2), OECD Guidelines for Multinational Enterprises (2011).

within six months from the adoption of the risk management plan and include qualitative and/or quantitative indicators to measure improvement.

D. Implement the risk management plan, monitor and track performance of risk mitigation, report back to designated senior management and consider suspending or discontinuing engagement with a refiner after their failed attempts at risk mitigation (pursuant to paragraphs 10 and 14 of Annex II of the Guidance) or corrective action to implement the due diligence recommendations in this Guidance.[48]

E. Undertake additional fact and risk assessments for risks requiring mitigation, or after a change of circumstances.[49] Supply chain due diligence is a dynamic process and requires on-going risk monitoring. After implementing a risk mitigation strategy, companies should repeat step 2 to ensure effective management of risk. Additionally, any change in the company's supply chain may require some steps to be repeated in order to prevent or mitigate adverse impacts.

48. Companies should suspend or discontinue engagement with the refiner (directly or through sub-suppliers) for a minimum of three months if within six months from the adoption of the risk management plan there is no significant measurable improvement made *i)* to prevent or mitigate the identified risk as described in paragraphs 10 and 14 of Annex II; or *ii)* in corrective action to implement the due diligence recommendations in this Guidance.
49. A change of circumstances should be determined on a risk-sensitive basis through on-going monitoring of the companies' chain of custody documentation and the contexts of the conflict-affected areas of mineral origin and transport. Such change of circumstances may include a change of supplier or actor in the chain of custody, place of origin, transportation routes or point of export. It may also include factors specific to the context, such as an increase in conflict in specific areas, changes in military personnel overseeing an area and ownership or control changes in the mine of origin.

STEP 4: CARRY OUT INDEPENDENT THIRD-PARTY AUDIT OF REFINER'S DUE DILIGENCE PRACTICES

OBJECTIVE: To carry out an independent third-party audit of the refiner's due diligence for responsible supply chains of gold from conflict-affected and high-risk areas and contribute to the improvement of refiner and upstream due diligence practices, including through any Institutionalised Mechanism or Industry Programme.

The recommendations in this section are not intended to be used as an audit standard but outline some basic principles, scope, criteria and other basic information for consideration by companies, Industry Programmes or any Institutionalised Mechanism to commission a supply chain-specific independent third-party audit of the implementation of the refiner's due diligence practices, either through new or pre-existing audit schemes. Auditors may rely on audit conclusions from other independent third party audits carried out for other purposes at points in the upstream supply chain (*e.g.* KYC audits or audits of bullion transporters), so long as those audits cover the areas as outlined below and are compliant with internationally recognised auditing standards for the assurance of management systems.[50]

A. **Plan an independent third party audit to verify the implementation of refiner's due diligence practices for responsible supply chains of gold from conflict-affected and high-risk areas.** The audit should include the following audit scope, criteria, principles and activities:[51]

1. **The scope of the audit:** The audit scope should include all activities, processes and systems used by the refiner to implement supply chain due diligence of gold from conflict-affected and high-risk areas. This includes, but is not limited to, relevant policies and procedures, refiner controls over the gold supply chain, communications with actors in the gold supply chain, the information disclosed to downstream companies on suppliers, chain of custody and other traceability information, refiner risk assessments including the on-the-ground research, and refiner strategies for risk management.

50. Examples of internationally recognised auditing standards include, but are not limited to, ISO19011, SA8000, ISAE 3000, and SSEA100.
51. Companies may consult ISO International Standard 19011: 2002 ("ISO 19011") for detailed requirements on audit programmes (including programme responsibilities, procedures, record-keeping, monitoring and reviewing) and a step-by-step overview of audit activities.

2. **The audit criteria:** The audit should determine the conformity of the implementation of refiner's due diligence practices against an audit standard that is based on this Guidance.
3. **The audit principles:**
   a) ***Independence:*** To preserve neutrality and impartiality of audits, the audit organisation and all audit team members ("auditors") must be independent from the refiner as well as from the refiner's subsidiaries, licensees, contractors, suppliers and companies cooperating in the joint audit. This means, in particular, that auditors must not have conflicts of interests with the auditee including business or financial relationships with the auditee (in the form of equity holdings, debt, securities), nor have provided services for the auditee company related to the design, establishment or implementation of the refiner's due diligence practices and/or that of the supply chain actors assessed therein, within a 24 month period prior to the audit.

   b) ***Competence:*** Auditors must have the personal attributes as well as scope specific competencies necessary to complete the third party audit. Companies may consult internationally recognised auditing standards[52] for detailed requirements on auditor competence when establishing new or revising pre-existing audit standards. Personal attributes should include, but are not limited to integrity, objectivity, confidentiality, open-mindedness, and professionalism. Scope specific competencies include, but are not limited to:

   i) Auditing principles, procedures and techniques.[53]

   ii) Supply chain due diligence principles, procedures and techniques.

   iii) Gold procurement practices and gold supply chains.

   iv) The social, cultural and historical contexts of the conflict-affected areas of gold origin or transport, including relevant linguistic abilities and culturally appropriate sensitivities for conducting audits.

   v) The OECD Guidance and Gold Supplement, including the model supply chain policy on minerals from conflict-affected and high-risk areas (Annex II).

   c) ***Accountability:*** An Industry Programmes or Institutionalised Mechanism should periodically review and monitor the ability of the auditors to carry out the audit in conformity with an audit programme, based on the

52. Examples of internationally recognised auditing standards include, but are not limited to, ISO19011, SA8000, ISAE 3000, and SSEA100.
53. Companies may consider existing management systems accreditations and completed auditor trainings such as ISO9001 or SA8000.

objectives, scope and criteria of the audit, judged against audit programme records.

4. **The audit activities:**

   a) ***Audit preparation:*** The objectives, scope, language and criteria for the audit should be clearly communicated to the auditors with any ambiguities clarified between the auditee and auditors before the initiation of the audit.[54] The auditors should determine the feasibility of the audit based on the availability of time, resources, information and cooperation of relevant parties.[55]

   b) ***In-site investigations:*** Before beginning the in-site investigations, auditors should prepare an audit plan,[56] and all working documents.[57] Auditors should gather further evidence and verify information by conducting *relevant interviews* (including interviews with management, as well as the assessment teams); *making observations*; and *reviewing documents (see below)*. In-site investigations should include:

      i) **The refiner facilities** and sites where the refiner carries out due diligence for responsible supply chains of gold from conflict-affected and high-risk areas.

      ii) **A sample of the refiner's suppliers** (including gold producers, local exporters, international gold traders, and recyclers) as may be required in accordance with the audit standard.

      iii) **Consultations with the assessment team(s)** which may be carried out remotely, to review the standards and methods for generating verifiable, reliable and up-to-date information.

      iv) Consultations with relevant local and central governmental authorities, and where they exist, UN expert groups, UN peacekeeping missions and local civil society, as determined by the auditor to be appropriate to the circumstances and risks identified in the gold supply chain.

   c) ***Document review:*** Samples of all documentation produced as part of the refiner's supply chain due diligence practices for gold from conflict affected areas should be reviewed "to determine the conformity of the system, as documented, with audit criteria."[58] This includes, but is not limited to, documentation on supply chain internal controls (a sample of chain of custody documentation, payment records), relevant

54. See Chapter 6.2 of ISO 19011.
55. Ibid.
56. See 6.4.1 of ISO 19011.
57. See 6.4.3 of ISO 19011.
58. See 6.3 of ISO 19011.

communications and contractual provisions with suppliers, documentation of information disclosed to downstream companies, evidence from the refiner's risk assessments (including all records on business partners and suppliers, interviews and on-the-ground assessments), and any documents on risk management strategies (*e.g.* agreements with suppliers on improvement indicators). Documentation should be sampled randomly by the auditors during the in-site investigation. Sample chosen should take into account *risks associated with suppliers and/or gold supply chains; peak and non-peak periods of the year; and volumes of material sourced from each supplier.* Documentation reviewed should include samples from each supplier as well as increase with the level of risk associated with business partners, suppliers or countries of origin of gold. Sample sizes should be increased if the auditor identifies concerns related to the refiner's due diligence measures.

d) ***Audit Conclusions:*** Auditors should generate findings that determine, based on the evidence gathered, the conformity of the refiner's due diligence practices for responsible supply chains of gold from conflict-affected and high-risk areas with the audit standard that is consistent with the recommendations of this section of the Guidance. Auditors should make recommendations in the audit report for the refiner to improve their due diligence practices Auditors should also prepare an audit summary report for publication in accordance with Step 5.

B. Implement the audit in accordance with the audit scope, criteria, principles and activities set out above. All actors in the supply chain should cooperate to ensure that the auditing is carried out in accordance with audit scope, criteria, principles and activities listed above. It is recommended that they do so through Industry Programmes or Institutionalised Mechanisms to carry out some or all of the following activities:

1. Draft Audit Standards in accordance with the recommendations of this Guidance.
2. Accredit auditors;
3. Oversee the audit programme, including a periodical review and monitoring of the ability of the auditors to carry out the audit in conformity with the audit programme;
4. Publish summary audit reports of refiners with due regard taken of business confidentiality and other competitive or security concerns. A summary audit report should include:
   a) Refiner details, the date of the audit and the audit period;
   b) The audit activities and methodology, as defined in Step 4(A)(4);

c) The audit conclusions, as defined in Step 4(A)(4), as they relate to each step in this Guidance

5. **SPECIFIC RECOMMENDATIONS – *For all upstream companies***

a) Allow access to company sites and relevant documentation and records of supply chain due diligence practices, in accordance with this Guidance.

b) Facilitate contact and logistics with transporters and suppliers selected by the audit team, and any consultations with stakeholders identified by the auditor.

c) If on-site visits of suppliers are required, facilitate contact and logistics.

6. **SPECIFIC RECOMMENDATIONS – *For all downstream companies***

a) It is recommended that downstream companies participate and support the independent third party audit of the refiner's due diligence practices, and are encouraged to do so through Industry Programmes to increase efficiency in the implementation of this guidance. This may include defining audit standards consistent with the recommendations set out in this Guidance. Small and medium enterprises are encouraged to join or build partnerships with such industry organisations.

STEP 5: REPORT ANNUALLY ON SUPPLY CHAIN DUE DILIGENCE

OBJECTIVE: To publicly report on due diligence for responsible supply chains of gold from conflict-affected and high-risk areas in order to generate public confidence in the measures companies are taking.

A. Annually report or integrate into annual sustainability or corporate responsibility reports, additional information on due diligence for responsible supply chains of gold from conflict-affected and high-risk areas, with due regard taken of business confidentiality and other competitive or security concerns.[59]

A.1. *For all upstream companies*

1. *Company Management Systems:* Report on steps taken to implement Step 1. Included in such reporting companies should set out the company's supply chain due diligence policy; explain the management structure responsible for the company's due diligence and who in the company is directly responsible; describe the internal systems of transparency, information collection and control over the gold supply chain from Step 1(C) and Step 3(B), explaining how this operates and how it has strengthened the company's due diligence efforts in the reporting period covered; describe the company's database and record keeping system and explain the methods for identifying all suppliers, down to the mine of origin and the methods for sharing the information about due diligence throughout the supply chain; disclose information on payments made to governments in line with EITI criteria and principles (where relevant).
2. *Company risk assessment in the supply chain:* Report on steps taken to implement Step 2. Included in such reporting, companies should explain how the company identified red flag operations or red flags in their supply chain, including the verifications of supplier representations proportional to risk; describe the red flags identified in the gold supply chain; describe the steps taken to map the factual circumstances of those red flag

59. Business confidentiality and other competitive or security concerns means, without prejudice to subsequent evolving interpretation: price information; supplier identities and relationships (however the identity of the refiner and the local exporter located in red flag locations should always be disclosed except in cases of disengagement); transportation routes; and the identity of information sources and whistle-blowers located in conflict-affected and high-risk areas, where revealing the identity of such sources would threaten their safety. All information will be disclosed to any institutionalised mechanism, regional or global, once in place with the mandate to collect and process information on minerals from conflict-affected and high-risk areas.

operations and red flagged supply chains; outline the methodology, practices and information yielded by the on-the-ground assessment team, including whether and how the company collaborated with other upstream companies, and how the company ensured that all joint work duly takes into consideration circumstances specific to the individual company; disclose the actual or potential risks identified. For the sake of clarity, companies should not report risks identified for potential suppliers with whom they have not done any business.

3. *Risk management:* Report on steps taken to implement Step 3. Included in such reporting, companies should describe how company internal control systems, such as chain of custody or traceability systems, have been strengthened to collect and maintain reliable up-to-date information on red flagged gold supply chains; describe the steps taken to manage risks, including a summary of the strategy for risk mitigation in the risk management plan, and capability-training, if any, and the involvement of affected stakeholders; disclose the efforts made by the company to monitor and track performance for risk mitigation and all the instances and results of follow-up after 6 months to evaluate significant and measurable improvement. Disclose the number of instances where the company has decided to disengage with suppliers and/or supply chains, consistent with Annex II, without disclosing the identity of those suppliers, except where the company deems it acceptable to do so in accordance with applicable laws. Companies should aim to report all instances of disengagement to relevant international and national investigative bodies and/or law enforcement authorities, having regard for the potential harmful effects of that reporting, and in accordance with applicable laws.

A.2. For refiners: In addition to the above, refiners should also:

1. *Audits:* Publish the summary audit reports of refiners with due regard taken of business confidentiality and other competitive or security concerns. The summary audit report should include:
   - *a)* Refiner details and the date of the audit;
   - *b)* The audit activities and methodology, as defined in Step 4(A)(4), where an Industry Programme or Institutionalised Mechanism in conformance with this Guidance and as defined in Step 4(B)(2) has not published these details;
   - *c)* The audit conclusions, as defined in Step 4(A)(4), as they relate to each step in this Guidance;

A.3. For all downstream companies

1. *Company Management Systems:* Report on steps taken to implement Step 1. Included in such reporting companies should set out the company's supply chain due diligence policy; explain the management structure responsible for the company's due diligence and who in the company is directly responsible; describe the control systems over the gold supply chain put in place by the company, explaining how this operates and how it has strengthened the company's due diligence efforts in the reporting period covered; describe the company's database and record-keeping system.
2. *Risk assessment:* Report on steps taken to implement Step 2. Included in such reporting, companies should describe the steps taken to identify refiners in their supply chain; describe the assessment of their due diligence practices; explain the methodology of company supply chain risk assessments; disclose the actual or potential risks identified.
3. *Risk management:* Report on steps taken to implement Step 3.[60] Included in such reporting, companies should describe the steps taken to manage risks, including a summary on the strategy for risk mitigation in the risk management plan, and capability-training, if any, and the involvement of affected stakeholders; disclose the efforts made by the company to monitor and track performance for risk mitigation and all the instances and results of follow-up after 6 months to evaluate significant and measurable improvement.

60. Publish additional audit reports or summaries, if any or if required by applicable laws, of the downstream company's due diligence practices with due regard taken of business confidentiality and other competitive or security concerns.

APPENDIX

Suggested measures to create economic and development opportunities for artisanal and small-scale miners

In conflict-affected and high-risk areas, artisanal and small-scale miners are particularly vulnerable to adverse impacts and serious abuses associated with the extraction, transport, trade, handling and export of gold. The vulnerability of artisanal and small-scale miners is increased when artisanal and small-scale mining operates in the absence of an enabling regulatory environment conducive to responsible, conflict-sensitive gold production and legitimate trade.

This Appendix aims to minimise the risk of marginalisation of the artisanal and small-scale mining sector, particularly the victims of extortion, while promoting conflict-free gold supply chains, thereby creating economic and development opportunities for artisanal and small-scale miners. This Appendix proposes measures to build secure, transparent and verifiable gold supply chains from mine to market and enable due diligence for legitimate ASM Gold to achieve these objectives, including through formalisation and legalisation efforts.

Governments, international organisations, donors, companies in the supply chain, and civil society organisations may consider the opportunity to explore collaborative ways to make use of these suggested options or other complementary approaches as they deem appropriate in accordance with national laws and policies.

1. **Assessment of mine sites consistent with the standards in Annex II of the OECD Due Diligence Guidance:**[61]

   a) Create, participate and support local multi-stakeholder commissions composed of focal points from civil society, industry and local and central government, to oversee the mine site assessment process:[62]

   i) develop clear parameters for assessing mine sites, transportation routes and points where gold is traded, consistent with the standards in Annex II of the OECD Due Diligence Guidance, and publish these parameters;[63]

ii) set up teams drawn from the multi-stakeholder commissions to assess mine sites based on these parameters, and publish results.

iii) focal points from multi-stakeholder commissions should solicit updated information through their on-the-ground networks on the conditions at mine sites, transportation routes and points where gold is traded. Information should be stored in a central clearinghouse. Information should be made available to assessment teams, government agencies, and upstream companies sourcing from the areas.

b) While considering the appropriate security options at mine sites:

i) disseminate this Guidance and make security forces aware of criminal and other penalties for illegal involvement in the extraction, trade, handling and export of gold; and

ii) support the formalisation of security arrangements between ASM communities, local government, and public or private security forces, in cooperation with civil society and international organisations, as appropriate, to ensure that all payments are freely made and proportionate to the service provided, clarify rules of engagement consistent with the Voluntary Principles on Security and Human Rights, the UN Code of Conduct for Law Enforcement Officials and the UN Basic Principles on the Use of Force and Firearms by Law Enforcement Officials.

2. **Formalisation of operations,**[64] including through:

a) Knowing the reasons for lack of formalisation in existing artisanal production and trading systems, in order to identify the best strategies for incentivising and enabling formalisation.

b) Providing technical assistance to help formalise artisanal and small-scale miners.

61. In the Great Lakes Region, this should be done through the national certification programs implementing the ICGLR Regional Certification Mechanism. See also the *Vision for Responsible Artisanal and Small-Scale Mining in Alliance for Responsible Mining* (Echavarria, C. *et. al.* Eds.), (2008) The Golden Vein – A guide to responsible artisanal and small-scale mining. ARM Series on Responsible ASM No. 1. Medellin.
62. See ICGLR Regional Certification Manual (2011).
63. See Appendix 3 and 4, ICGLR Certification Manual (2011).
64. See Rock Solid Chances, Felix Hruschka and Cristina Echavarría, Alliance for Responsible Mining (2011), available at *http://www.communitymining.org/index.php/en/arm-publications*. In the Great Lakes Region, see the fourth tool of the ICGLR Regional Initiative against the Illegal Exploitation of Natural Resources, "Formalisation of the Artisanal Mining Sector".

c) Acknowledging the diversity in the types and sizes of artisanal and small-scale mining activity.

d) Creating and participating in collaborative initiatives to establish the modalities and financing of support funds to assist with the formalisation process.[65]

3. **Legalisation of operations.**[66] Assist artisanal and small-scale miners to obtain mining rights and other related authorisations through legitimate processes. Consider other regulatory measures to legalise operations of artisanal and small-scale miners. Where there are challenges regarding illegal mining on mining concessions, all stakeholders concerned are encouraged to facilitate constructive dialogue between title holders and artisanal and small-scale producers, where those parties are acting in good faith. In case of title disputes, mediated solutions should be sought through cooperation with government and other stakeholders.

4. **Assessment of trading hubs and regular mapping of transportation routes:**

a) Set up and participate in teams drawn from the multi-stakeholder commissions (see above) to annually assess points where gold is traded and transportation routes based on the parameters laid out above.

65. See Responsible Jewellery Council, Standards Guidance, "COP 2.14 Artisanal and Small-Scale Mining", which lists the following analogous opportunities for large-scale mining and ASM initiatives: "Providing financing (loans) for technical and other improvements; Assisting and training miners on a range of issues (for example, occupational health, reclamation, mining and processing methods, value added processes, organisational and financial management, explosives management); Aiding miners in the determination of mineral reserves (combined with support for access to financing); Providing emergency response services; Availing processing services to miners or building their capacity to implement effective processing facilities themselves with improved technology; Liaising with government departments, NGOs, trade unions and international agencies to obtain additional support; Providing guidance on marketing and commercialisation, including fair trade arrangements; Proactively supporting alternative livelihoods, economic development, and other improvements in ASM communities; Supporting the wider community by locally sourcing the provision of as many goods and services as possible; Eliminating child labor as a condition of engagement in the community; Improving women's conditions in ASM communities through gender awareness and empowerment programs."
66. Responsible artisanal and small-scale mining comply with national legal frameworks. When the applicable legal framework is not enforced, or in the absence of such a framework, the good faith efforts of artisanal and small-scale miners and enterprises to operate within the applicable legal framework (where it exists) as well as their engagement in opportunities for formalisation as they become available (bearing in mind that in most cases, artisanal and small-scale miners have very limited or no capacity, technical ability or sufficient financial resources to do so) should be taken into account.

b) To avoid any potential contamination of sources, construct and maintain secure depots at major points where gold is traded. In considering the appropriate security options at points where gold is traded and along transportation routes:

i) disseminate this Guidance and make security forces aware of criminal and other penalties for illegal involvement in the extraction, trade, handling and export of gold; and

ii) support the formalisation of security arrangements between ASM communities, local government, and public or private security forces, in cooperation with civil society and international organisations, as appropriate, to ensure that all payments are freely made and proportionate to the service provided, clarify rules of engagement consistent with the Voluntary Principles on Security and Human Rights, the UN Code of Conduct for Law Enforcement Officials and the UN Basic Principles on the Use of Force and Firearms by Law Enforcement Officials;

5. **Establishment of traceability and/or chain of custody systems that ensures security of shipments and enables data collection on all gold from assessed mine sites.** It is recommended that the assessment of mine sites is immediately followed by the introduction of sound chain of custody or traceability systems. Chain of custody and/or traceability systems should progressively collect and maintain information for every gold shipment from assessed mine sites.[67]

6. **Providing financial support to *i)* multi-stakeholder commissions to assess mine sites, transportation routes and points where gold is traded; and *ii)* chain of custody and/or traceability schemes.** Financial support may take on a variety of forms, including direct support to initiatives, or royalties and premiums on gold from assessed mines and transportation routes with chain of custody and/or traceability systems in place.

7. **Promoting and taking part in programs to directly and competitively market ASM gold from assessed mine sites.** Facilitate contacts and build partnerships between artisanal and small-scale producers operating on assessed mine sites, smelter/refiners, direct marketing of gold from assessed mine sites passing through secure and verifiable transportations routes.

8. **Support the establishment of a grievance mechanism**, consistent with Step 1(E) of this Supplement, and take steps to enable artisanal and

67. For a detailed list of information that should be included in chain of custody and/or traceability systems as they relate to specific minerals, see Step 2(C) of the *Supplement on Gold*.

small-scale producers to access this mechanism so they may alert companies and government authorities of concerns related to the extraction, transport, trade, handling and export of gold from conflict-affected and high-risk areas.

9. **Fostering cooperation between customs authorities of exporting and importing countries.**

ORGANISATION FOR ECONOMIC CO-OPERATION AND DEVELOPMENT

The OECD is a unique forum where governments work together to address the economic, social and environmental challenges of globalisation. The OECD is also at the forefront of efforts to understand and to help governments respond to new developments and concerns, such as corporate governance, the information economy and the challenges of an ageing population. The Organisation provides a setting where governments can compare policy experiences, seek answers to common problems, identify good practice and work to co-ordinate domestic and international policies.

The OECD member countries are: Australia, Austria, Belgium, Canada, Chile, the Czech Republic, Denmark, Estonia, Finland, France, Germany, Greece, Hungary, Iceland, Ireland, Israel, Italy, Japan, Korea, Luxembourg, Mexico, the Netherlands, New Zealand, Norway, Poland, Portugal, the Slovak Republic, Slovenia, Spain, Sweden, Switzerland, Turkey, the United Kingdom and the United States. The European Union takes part in the work of the OECD.

OECD Publishing disseminates widely the results of the Organisation's statistics gathering and research on economic, social and environmental issues, as well as the conventions, guidelines and standards agreed by its members.

OECD PUBLISHING, 2, rue André-Pascal, 75775 PARIS CEDEX 16
(20 2016 02 1 P) ISBN 978-92-64-25238-7 – 2016